MIME
The Step Beyond Words

MIME
The Step Beyond Words

FOR THE ACTORS OF DANCE AND DRAMA

(Revised Edition)

by Adrian Pecknold

Preface by Michael Langham

NC Press Limited

Toronto, 1989

Acknowledgements
I am indebted to the following generous people who contributed in so many ways to bring this book to publication:
Jacques Lecoq, Michael Langham, John Hirsch, Jean Gascon, Myra Benson, Alex Nagy, Preston Haskell, Tom Hendry, Caroline Walker, Theatre Arts students and teachers across Canada and the members of the Canadian Mime Theatre and the International Mime Community.

to

Gwen Hewlings	*who opened the gate*
Yvonne Green	*who led us down the novice path*
Myra Benson	*who marked the pitfalls*
Jacques Lecoq	*who expanded the horizons*
Brian Doherty	*who was the catalyst*
Alex Nagy	*who defined the boundaries*
my wife Addie	*who shared the loneliness*
and associates	*who have deep pride in their profession and know the word "share" to mean both give and take,*

my deepest gratitude.

Canadian Catalogue Publication Data
Pecknold, Adrian 1920-
  Mime

Rev. ed.
Bibliography: p.
ISBN 1-55021-037-8

1. Mime.   I. Title.

PN2071.G4P43 1989   792.3'02   C88-095200-8

We would like to thank the Ontario Arts Council and the Canada Council for their assistance in the production of this book.

New Canada Publications, NC Press Limited, Box 4010, Stn. A, Toronto, ON, Canada M5W 1H8.

Cover: Illustration from "The Lamplighter" Series,
Photographs:
    Cover and demonstration photographs by Alex Nagy
    Production photographs by Preston Haskell

Contents

Part III   Illusory Techniques

Part IV   Solos, Ensembles, Mimodrama

Preface by Michael Langham

In the mid-sixties, when Adrian Pecknold was a member of the Stratford Festival Company of Canada, I remember being quite unnerved by his apparent disinterest in the speaking of Shakespeare's text. It wasn't that he couldn't appreciate the meanings of the words or the evocative implications of the phrases — he comprehended it all very thoroughly — but he clearly found the language itself (i.e., Shakespeare) a very real encumbrance to his creative instinct. This invariably expressed itself in a non-verbal, physical language that made the lines alarmingly redundant!

At that early date it was already apparent that here was a significant mime-artist in the making. Now, in the early-eighties, Adrian Pecknold has long established himself as a leading exponent of the subject — both as practitioner and teacher — with an enviable reputation. It is therefore a great luxury for lovers of the performing arts to have some of this magical know-how displayed in a book. The book not only opens the door to a tantalizing and much-neglected world in the stage-performer's art; it also makes the practice of it vividly clear for student and teacher.

Michael Langham

Adrian Pecknold

Adrian Pecknold is best known for his mime character 'Poco' appearing for the past twenty years on the long-running Canadian children's television show, "Mr. Dressup." He is the definitive 'Lucky' in Beckett's *Waiting for Godot*, having played the part at Manitoba Theatre Centre in Winnipeg, Manitoba, CBC Television's "Festival" series and his exquisite interpretation of the role according to theatre critic and director Urjo Kareda at Stratford Festival Theatre in 1968.

In 1969, Adrian founded The Canadian Mime Theatre at Niagara-on-the-Lake. He was the Artistic Director, Writer and Lead Mime for eight years and founded The Canadian Mime Theatre School.

Under his direction the School represented Canada at the ASSITEJ International Festival in Sofia, Bulgaria. Their tremendous success there resulted in numerous invitations to appear internationally. Over the following eight years, Adrian took his company on tour several times across Canada and the U.S.A., three times to Europe and a most prestigious tour around the world to Fiji, New Zealand, Australia, Singapore, Scotland and England to international acclaim in 1976. In 1977 Adrian Pecknold was the recipient of the Queens' Silver Jubilee Medal for his contribution to theatre in Canada.

Adrian has received several awards for acting and directing over the years in Canadian professional theatre. He created the title role in Ken Mitchell's *Davin, The Politician* at Regina's Globe Theatre. He played 'Phil' in *Jitters* for ten weeks at Stage West Edmonton. He created and played the Clown in a show for the First International Festival of Clowning at Dartmouth, Nova Scotia. He has created and produced Mime Shows for the International Trade Fair at Chicago, the International Auto Show at Toronto and the Art Galley of Ontario.

He spends the fall semester teaching acting and mime at both the University of Guelph and Ryerson Theatre School in Toronto. As a member of the Theatre Ontario Talent Bank he is much sought after as a director, play polisher and instructor of workshops in Mask, Mime and Movement throughout Ontario.

His book, *Mime, The Step Beyond Words* was first published in 1982 by NC Press Limited of Toronto. It was reprinted in 1985, and a revised and enlarged edition is being re-published in 1989.

Foreword by the Author

While touring centres in the Northwest Territories and numerous cities and towns across the rest of Canada, both performing and conducting mime workshops for teachers and students, I became aware of the pressing need for a plainly-written text on the subject of mime, this resurging form of theatre which has been so neglected in the past.

After a performance or workshop inevitably I was asked, "Where can I find books on the techniques of mime? Where can I find written plays or mime pieces?"

This book is directed to the teacher and student of theatre arts, now standard fare in many high schools, vocational colleges and universities. It is directed as well to the teacher and student of professional theatre and dance, whose formal training may have been neglected in the skills of mime.

It will be impossible to deal with the broad subject of theatre and its many areas exhaustively. However, *Mime: The Step Beyond Words* will serve as an introduction to the basic concepts of mime from the point of view of the performer.

There is a natural progression from Part I through Part IV. However, selected material may be chosen from each section to constitute one class period. Further selections may be added as the term progresses along with a constant review of the previous material.

Part I begins by outlining the very important neutral position, and immediately proceeds to some special mime exercises and a few essential tumbling routines, introducing the student to a different approach to body control and grace of movement which will eventually build in him or her a strong sense of confidence. The exercises are designed to strengthen seldom-used muscles and to develop coordination and control. Warm-up exercises are not included in the book but should always be done at the beginning of class.

From this preparatory stage, we progress in Part II to the more specific techniques of using the hands, arms and shoulders, and introducing the dynamic of mime.

Part III deals with the more complicated, traditional, illusory mime techniques. These techniques build on the combined physical and mental approach the student has been working toward in earlier sections.

Finally there is part IV, a revised section of mime pieces which I wrote and produced for the Canadian Mime Theatre. The themes are first presented in an abbreviated précis form. Each is then followed by a more developed presentation of the same piece, will indicate ways in which an idea or situation may progress from an initial concept to the final polished piece. For the new edition we have added new mime pieces.

Teachers may wish to revise the order of presentation or omit the précis in some instances.

It is a great pleasure to make this book available again in an expanded format. Thanks to all my students and colleagues who have worked with me.

Adrian Pecknold

The Definition

There is some controversy over the meaning and uses of the words "mime" and "pantomime" and the words derived from them. I prefer to think of them as synonymous and most people use them interchangeably. The Living Webster Dictionary implies the degree of sameness of the two words.

> *Mime, n. (L. mimus, Gr. mimos, imitator, actor, mime or farce)* A mimic; an actor or comedian specializing in pantomime or mimicry; the art of narration or portrayal of character, idea or mood by bodily movements; pantomime; a kind of farce popular among the ancient Greeks and Romans etc. etc.

> *Pantomime, n. (L. pantomimus, Gr. pantomimos, panto, all and mimos, imitator, E. mime.)* The dramatic technique of communicating through mute gestures; gesture without speech etc. etc.

The English Christmas Pantomime is quite apart from the form we are considering and should always be referred to as Christmas Pantomime or English Pantomime, to avoid confusion. It is a theatrical spectacle featuring singing, dancing and comical skits usually adapted from fairy tales. The familiar contraction or diminutive of the English reference to Pantomime is, strangely enough, "Panto" and not "Mime."

Part I
The Basic Concepts

The Bauhaus L-Boxes

The year I founded the Canadian Mime Theatre I had been reading an article about the Bauhaus movement in design and the very simplicity on which that concept is based inspired me to design what I have called the Bauhaus Box.

I have found their very simple formality so adaptable and flexible that I would like to pass it on.

Each box is shaped in an L-shape, and each dimension is a multiple of whatever basic dimension you chose. I have found twenty centimetres to be very practical.

Each L-Box can be used independently or may lock into another L-Box to become a rectangle. I would recommend a set of six L-Boxes. Plywood, reinforced at the right-angled joins, is a good strong construction.

They can simulate chairs, tables, benches, lounges, love seats, theatre seats, dentist chairs, walls, machinery, cars . . . you name it: you believe it: you use it in that fashion: . . . then we will believe it.

In the Beginning

Imagine early man before the evolution of verbal symbols and the invention of language. Imagine his need and desire to communicate. He must underline and dramatize his gutteral sounds by inventing hand signs and gestures, by adopting physical attitudes, by imitating animals and inanimate objects, by acting out the needs of the moment. By mimicry he can fortell future events and relate past happenings, portray the awesomeness of natural phenomena, and create ritualistic ceremonies of appeasement and thanksgiving to his gods. Add to this the natural rhythms of the theme, the musicality of the imitated sounds, and we can readily accept these imaginary scenes as the aboriginal roots of mime and dance — dramatic movement *per se.*

From this imagined historical perspective, it is quite easy to believe that mime is inherent in us all.

The late Nathan Cohen, a most respected Canadian drama critic, when reviewing the first season of the Canadian Mime Theatre which I founded in the summer of 1969 at Niagara-on-the-Lake, Ontario, gave the following historical background.

"The tradition of mime goes back more than 2,500 years and can be found in all cultures. Mime was developed to a fine art in ancient Greece. In Roman times, mime flourished in the colony of Syracuse, and was enormously popular at festivals. Indeed, in Rome, many exponents of mime achieved wealth and position. Of course, wealth had its perils. Paris was executed by Nero for being his professional superior. There being nothing really new in theatre, nudity was permitted in mime shows. Some emperors encouraged the realistic performance of everything from intercourse to execution. Not surprisingly, the Christian church had very little use for mime and by the fifth century A.D., it (mime) was out of official favour.

"But mime was too popular and useful to be extinguished. It lived on and even survived the Dark Ages to become Commedia dell'Arte. Its influence can be seen in the works of Shakespeare, Molière, Lopé de Vega and many others. This heritage produced some of its finest exponents in twentieth century silent film: Charlie Chaplin, Max Linder, Buster Keaton, Harry Langdon, and Laurel and Hardy were all superb mimes. However much the work has changed, certain emotions and attitudes remain the same, and they are the impulse power of the mimetic art."

Historically, mime received its greatest thrust from the mid-fifteenth to the mid-nineteenth century. During this renaissance, mime flourished in Italy. The popular theatre of the day was a roisterous, vulgar and farcical form called *Commedia dell'Arte*. It was performed in the market squares and court yards by acting companies which travelled from village to village. They became known as the Italian Strolling Players and were sometimes referred to as the *Funambuli*.

This was an improvisational form of theatre, both spoken and mimed. During this period literally hundreds of stock characters were created: Arlecchino, Columbine, Pantalone, Dottore, Capitano, Isabella, Lelio, Pulcinella, and Pedrolino to name just a few. They became so popular with the masses that they were handed down to younger friends or relatives as the actors outgrew the roles, thus continuing the tradition. Most of them, except for the romantic lovers and the women characters, were performed in half-mask.

The Strolling Players travelled far afield, having a profound and lasting effect on theatre in the countries they visited.

The English Punch, the ever popular puppet Punch of Punch and Judy fame, is a direct descendant of the *Commedia*. The prototype was Pulcinella, who had a tremendous hooked nose and a hump-back and wore a tall, pointed hat just as Punch does today. The dress of Pantalone, red breeches and stockings, has been passed down to us as pantaloons, and finally, pants.

The character of Arlecchino became the more romanticized Harlequin in the hands of French actors who also took the rather stupid character, Pedrolino, and made him the poignant, melancholy and sentimental Pierrot. Indeed, Jean Gaspard Deburau became the most popular actor in France, playing the role of Pierrot in the pantomimes at the *Théâtre de Funambules* in Paris, from 1816 until his death in 1846. It was Deburau who first attempted to de-emphasize the face by coating it with white flour.

With the death of the great Deburau, the mime tradition struggled on for eighty years or more with diminishing success.

Mime, as it is practiced today, developed in the early part of this century from one theatre school. It would later evolve into two broad and different philosophies based on aesthetic preferences rather than conflicting evaluations of technical difficulty.

The initial exploration began in 1921, under the direction of the noted French critic and teacher Jacques Copeau, when he founded *L'École du Vieux-Colombier* in Paris. Here, Étienne Decroux, Jean-Louis Barrault, Jean Dasté, Jean Dorcy and others, were to explore, through the use of mask, what were to become the exercises and technique of the new mime. The school was disbanded in 1924, but a beginning had been made. The careers of those involved in the earlier experiments were to carry mime in two different directions over the years that followed.

Étienne Decroux, with Jean-Louis Barrault, explored a thrust of ''pure'' mime, which became what is now referred to as ''Mime Corporeal.'' Decroux agreed with the attempt to de-emphasize the face and use the body only, as a means of expression.

Marcel Marceau, a student of Decroux's, also used the white face for his character ''Bip.'' Marceau's tremendous international popularity at one time had the public thinking that all mimes wore the white mask of grease paint.

The alternate thrust came from Jean Dasté, who, after the demise of the Vieux-Colombier, continued to act and teach and write, furthering the concepts of the new mime as a part of general acting technique.

Jacques Lecoq, a student of Jean Dasté, continued to explore the use of mask and mime. For a period of eight years he was *Maître de Mime* of the Teatro Piccolo de Milano, Italy. This is one of the last great companies still practicing the traditional *Commedia dell' Arte*. Jacques Lecoq later returned to Paris, and in 1956 established his own school of mime and theatre. His methods have become what is now referred to as ''Mime for the Actor.''

École Jacques Lecoq was my alma mater, and the exercises and technique described in this book are the result. Other Canadians have since gone to Lecoq and returned to Canada to further his teaching, and, today perhaps, the Lecoq theories predominate in the Canadian mime scene.

Decroux, also, continues to teach in Paris, and many of his students have returned to Canada to work. The two schools of thought live in reasonable harmony, both spreading the ''word'' of mime.

Other wonderful teachers have passed their insights on to me. I hope that I have expounded them in such a way that they will be meaningful to you.

It has been my pleasure to work with, and teach mime to members of the Stratford Festival Theatre, Toronto Workshop Productions, the Royal Winnipeg Ballet, the Toronto Dance Theatre, the Canadian Brass, Camarata, Doug Henning, Sylvia Tyson, seminars of music teachers, physical education teachers and a great number of my fellow actors. Without exception, the enthusiasm and inspiration their work with mime stimulated has been to me a very rewarding experience.

The international acceptance of the work for which I have been responsible, gave me the confidence, and the kind assistance of the Canada Council gave me the necessary resources to proceed with the book.

The Approach

Mime looks deceptively simple. As in all beautifully and painstakingly simplified artforms, the amount of training and practice needed to acquire competence is indeed great. Too often the neophyte is attracted to the profession by its apparent simplicity and is not prepared to devote the time and effort required to become at least proficient in the technique. Too often he or she rushes headlong into performance and the result is like an importunate child.

Just as the musician must know his instrument, practise hour upon tedious hour, scale after similar scale, gradually strengthening his embouchure and the dexterity of his fingers, searching for the exact vibrato to bring out the best of his particular tone, and observing life as he lives and sees others live it, developing his sensitivity to the rhythms and phrasing in one heightened moment of musical communication — so must the mime know his instrument, his body. He must practise hour after tedious hour, exercise after similar exercise, gradually strengthening the seldom-used muscles, separating and isolating the physical movements, finding the exact muscular tone to suit the action, observing life as he lives and sees others live it, developing his sensitivity to the rhythms and physical phrasing in one heightened moment of dramatic communication.

The more one is exposed to other forms of art, the more meaningful one's own discipline becomes.

The Physical Institution

There is an abundance of historical writing on the development of the dramatic arts from simple campfire communal gatherings to the sophisticated institution we now call "theatre." A dramatic presentation requires a setting or locale of some kind. Of the various structural forms with which different societies have experimented, the one that has persisted throughout the ages is the proscenium arch stage. This design is eminently suited to the presentation of mime, because the performance must go out to the audience in unrestricted sight lines. Every action and every gesture of every mime character must be seen by every member of the audience.

It has been said that theatre is the bringing together of actors and audience, both of whom, for a period of time, are prepared to suspend their disbelief. The audience will become involved with the actors who essentially believe that they are the characters they portray and that the stage is the place it purports to be. The mime is particularly favoured in this respect, since he can suggest the illusion of any environment, of any number of characters, and of any properties which might be required without their having concrete substance, simply by his use of space and the substance of space.

The Neutral Inner State

Just as a musician's instrument lies dormant and soundless in a neutral but perfectly tuned state, ready to produce the exact note the composer has written, so must the mime's instrument, his body, be in a neutral state, alert and yet relaxed, ready to respond with the exact nuance the playwright requires.

This neutral state is a matter of degree. Life is experienced in a relative sense. Our ways of experiencing, physical, emotional and mental, fluctuate from inertness to extreme activity. We can be tired or bursting with energy; stuffed up with a head cold or breathing deeply the fragrance of a spring day; overcome by bereavement or ecstatic with a special happiness; bored and uninterested or inquiring and restless.

Within this spectrum lies a state of well-being which, although not openly expressed, is charged with that degree of static energy which has so much to do with stage presence. It is best described as the Neutral Inner State.

The Neutral Inner State is as important as activity; all action or reaction stems from it and inevitably returns to it.

The Neutral Outer State

In order to ''act'' from the Neutral Inner State, the mime must express his inner state of being outwardly, the Neutral Outer State. It is up to him to decide how much of his inner feeling he will transfer to outer action: To what degree will he need to transmit his thoughts and sensory perceptions into physical and emotional expression?

The dramatic situation as related to the actor's personal life will usually evoke the appropriate response. However, experience teaches that everything in theatre must be slightly larger than life in order to project believably from the stage. As mimes, words are denied us; we must find physical symbols to take the place of verbal symbols. We must outwardly manifest our inner state by attitude, position, manipulation or movement, be it a flick of an eyebrow, an intake of breath, a slackening of the jaw, a widening of the eyes, a curve of the lip, a stifled yawn or a back flip.

However, before we begin movement, let us describe the Neutral Outer State in simple muscular terms.

Stand with the feet comfortably apart. Allow a lifting feeling to flow through your body, beginning in the stomach or groin area, and rising, up through the chest, to escape through the collar bone area, just below the voice box. This area, around your collar bone, is called ''the point of levity,'' after Viola Spolin.

Lift your rib cage slightly as this feeling becomes more positive. Keep your arms relaxed and hanging comfortably from your shoulders, which also should be relaxed. Breathe slowly and comfortably from the diaphragm, not allowing the rib cage to heave or move unnaturally. Make sure that the neck muscles are relaxed by slowly turning your head from side to side and forward again. Think in vertical terms and check that you have slightly drawn in the abdominal muscles to give them a firm tone.

Wherever possible, any physical exercise or technique should begin and end with the neutral state.

The Leading Centre

We have just described the Neutral Outer State and the vertical, symmetrical feeling based on a central point which we have called the point of levity. If you move forward from this neutral state, you will find that it leads you to walk in the most natural and symmetrical, i.e. neutral, fashion possible. The whole body is responding to this symmetry: it is following the Leading Centre. Stanislavsky speaks of moving by leading with a physical part of the body, for example, a left ear or a right shoulder.

It can readily be seen how a Leading Centre placed elsewhere, say at the left hip, produces certain asymmetrical motions. These motions are called ''shadow moves.''

This can be a preliminary approach to exploring the physical movements peculiar to a particular character, perhaps, as in the above example, one with a stiff left leg. The rest of the body responds naturally with the appropriate shadow moves and a very realistic character is created in purely physical terms.

To repeat, a Leading Centre placed at the point of levity allows you to move in a symmetrical fashion; a leading centre placed elsewhere forces you to move in an asymmetrical fashion.

Peripheral Vision

The properties of mass in space, the motion of spatial form, and the acuteness of one's peripheral vision are extremely important to the mime. From the moment he enters any area, the mime, who has especially trained himself to relate physically to surrounding objects, becomes aware of his position relative to the larger obvious forms: first to other people, furniture, windows, doors; then to bright colours, light sources, and smaller objects; and then to helpful topographical features such as spills, stains, knot-holes, carpets and design features. Finally, he must be aware of arbitrarily-placed stage spikes.

Just as a painter must assess his canvas and decide where his forms will be placed, so must the actor balance his canvas, the stage: symmetrically if he is in harmony with the situation; or asymmetrically, if he is at discord with it. A heightened visual sense will help the mime adjust his positioning relative to other actors and objects on stage.

Most often cues are given and received visually in mime pieces, although in some situations it is not possible to look directly at the person who is giving the physical cue. In an instance such as this it is surprising how much one ca_____ed and strengthened periph_____

R____ your hand____el to the sides of you_____ from your ears. Lo_____aw your hands back un_____es to your line of vi_____or wiggle your fingers a_____can read this motion. _____ be more aware of _____is area of extended

Audience Focus

If the audience is to be completely at ease and able to follow the important moments on stage, it must know where and when to look for them.

In a spoken play, much of the plot is conveyed through the inflection, tone and the actual words within the dialogue. The focus most naturally goes from speaker to speaker until the playwright or the director employs some other technique to attract the attention of the audience.

In a mime play there are no audible verbal symbols to attract the audience's focus. We must use movement or its opposite, non-movement, to catch the eye. If there is a great deal of movement at different points at the same time on stage, the audience will be unable to read meaning into it and begin to resent the intrusions and lose interest in the play.

In order to focus the attention of the audience on major moves and gestures, there must first be a time of minimal movement. Actors must first learn to be still and to find within themselves both the physical neutral and the inner neutral states. This charged stillness generates a static energy from which any movement, however minute, will immediately attract attention. (Conversely, in a very busy and active situation, a character who remains still will, by his very stillness, attract attention.)

Actions and reactions may now easily be read and interpreted, and relationships and situations will be clearly understandable. Movement must be meaningful and economical in the extreme, and yet ''theatrical'' enough to project beyond the footlights at the edge of the stage.

Special Exercises

Many texts dealing with movement contain excellent exercises and set routines. Here are a few special exercises which are not always included in such texts but which are of particular benefit to the mime. These exercises will develop a heightened degree of flexibility and of that strength and muscle power or muscular energy which we will refer to as "tone." Tone in the muscles can encompass the full range from complete relaxation to an extremely heightened degree of preparedness or a readiness to move in any given direction at any given moment.

These exercises will also develop muscle co-ordination, and muscle isolation or separation (the ability to call on one muscle to perform a function in isolation from surrounding muscles and to separate one muscle or group of muscles from others). They require that we extend certain muscles in a more elongated manner than we are used to, and conversely that we compact the muscles in a more contracted manner than usual.

It is desirable to establish a certain form which will give structure to our efforts. This form, in the guise of certain principles, will become apparent as the text progresses. Later, if and when we wish to break these patterns, we will be aware of our departure from these basic forms or principles.

Before we start our exercises, then, let us establish a structure.

Preparation: Think out the demands that will be made of the body throughout the exercise from the beginning to the end. Determine the neutral inner and outer states of preparedness.

Execution: Physically activate these demands to the degree required, taking care that movements be neither overstated nor understated.

Completion: Return to the neutral inner and outer state of preparedness.

Relaxation: Completely relax the body for a few brief moments.

A short physical warm-up should precede the following exercises.

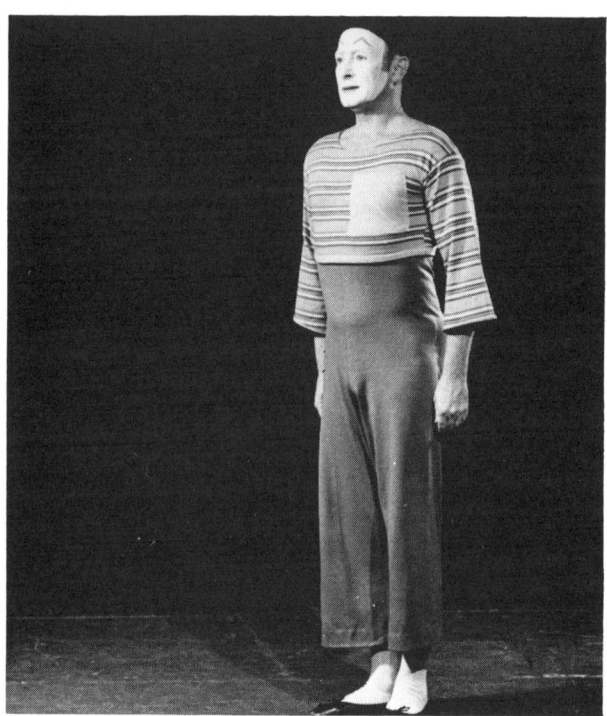

Figure 1

Figure 2

The Cat Jump

Starting in the neutral physical state (figure 1), bend your knees and slowly lower your body vertically to gently kneel on both knees at the same time (figures 2 and 3). Extend your toes and sit lightly on your heels (figure 4), hands resting on your thighs. Your point of levity should be working, giving a heightened vertical feeling to your upper body.

Extend your arms in front of you. Find a point on the horizon and concentrate on it visually (figure 5). Mentally anticipate the degree of energy that will be required to lift your sitting body vertically off the floor to a height sufficient to allow your legs to extend from underneath and to permit you to be able to land, flat footed, in a half crouch position with your arms extended in front to assist you in attaining absolute stillness and perfect balance.

Figure 4

Figure 3

Figure 5

Concentrate, and, when you are ready physically, execute this action by drawing on the energy that you have mentally summoned, giving your body the impulse "up." Hold the half crouch position for a count of four in perfect balance and stillness (figure 6).

Stand slowly, lowering your arms to your sides, maintaining awareness of the point of levity as you return to the neutral position (figure 7), and relax.

The count of four mentioned above is particularly important in judging whether the movement has been well executed. If you overestimate the energy required, you will fall forward during this count; if you underestimate it, you will fall backward.

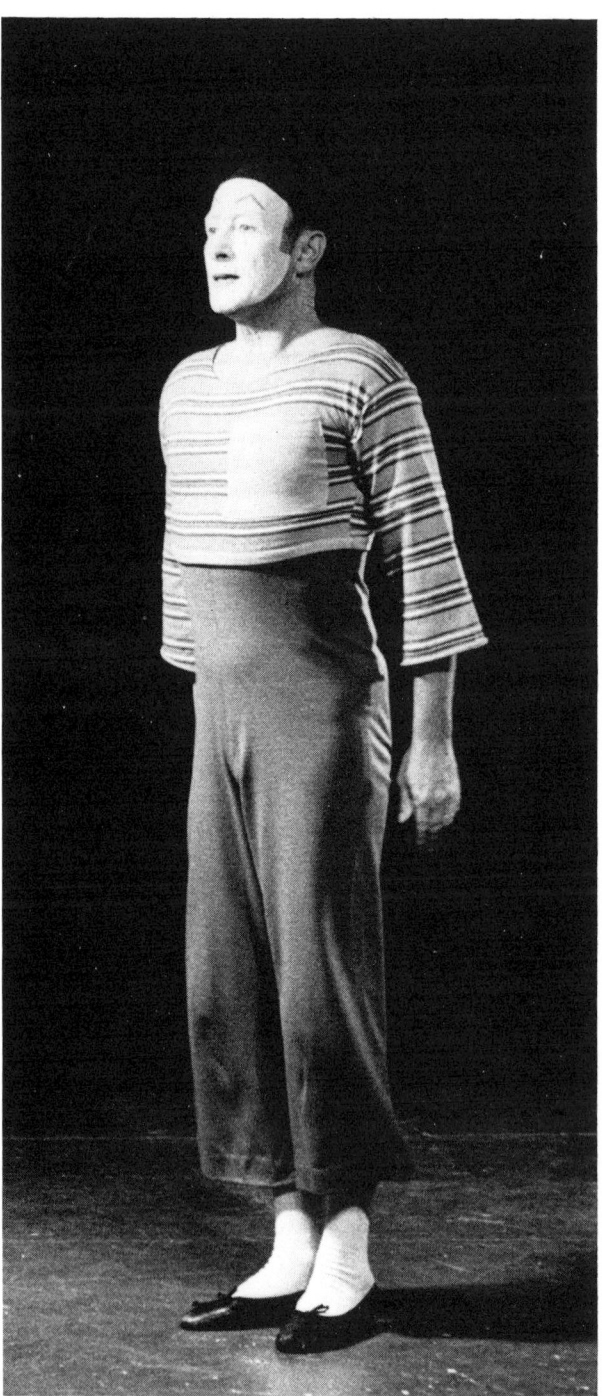

Figure 7

Figure 6

The Star

Start from the neutral position with your point of levity operating. To assist in balance, extend your arms to either side level with your shoulders. Keeping your head up, lean forward from the waist. At the same time extend one leg back, elongating your body parallel to the floor, keeping perfect balance.

Now, bending the knee of the supporting leg, lower your body until your lower abdomen rests on your thigh (figure 8). Slowly return to a standing position and repeat the exercise using the other leg as the base.

Figure 8

The Bird

Repeat the Star exercise to the point demonstrated in figure eight. Now, maintaining your balance, undulate your arms from the shoulders through the elbows, wrists, and hands like a bird in flight. Bank your arms into left and right soaring turns, allowing the supporting foot to adjust to the slight directional changes.

You might combine the Cat Jump and the Bird exercises, for example, into an impression of an eagle sitting on its nest, being startled into flight, and returning to the nest.

The most accomplished students could try jumping from the Cat Jump directly onto one balancing foot and going immediately into the bird impression.

The Pendulum

Begin from the neutral position. With your knees slightly bent, swing your arms from the shoulders, forward and backward, quite relaxed. Each time the arms go forward or backward, rock up onto the balls of the feet (figures 9 and 10). Do this for a count of eight beats.

Rest one arm, when it is forward, for one beat and then continue to swing your arms alternately, forward and back (figure 11). Again count eight.

On the eighth beat, without stopping or breaking the rhythm, swing the arm that is extended behind you out to the side and then force it to swing back in front of you, along the plane which the body is facing, side to side in one continuous motion (figure 12). The other arm will continue to swing forward and backward alternately to the arm that is now swinging to the side and at a right angle to it (figure 13). Continue this pattern as well for a count of eight beats.

Figure 9

Figure 11

Figure 10

Figure 12

Figure 13

Return to the forward and backward alternating swinging for a further eight beats (figure 14).

Repeat the side-swinging configuration, this time using the opposite arm for eight beats.

Once again return to the forward and backward alternating swinging, again for eight beats. Throughout the whole of this exercise to this point, continue to rock up onto the balls of the feet in time with the swinging.

Now, without breaking the rhythm, do not allow the arms to swing back downward; instead make them continue in the directions they are going so that each one completes a circle up, over the head (figures 15, 16, 17 and 18) and down again into the alternating swing, forward and backward.

During this overhead manoeuvre, elongate the body as the arms reach overhead, and stretch onto the balls of the feet (figure 16). Cease rocking the feet for a count of four beats until the pattern is completed. Also, note that the shoulders turn slightly to each side.

Figure 14

Figure 15

Figure 16

Figure 17

Figure 18

Complete the phrase by resuming the rocking of the feet and the swinging of the arms forward and backward for four beats (figures 19 and 20).

Finally, repeat the last manoeuvre with the arms going in the opposite direction to the previous time. Finish the exercise by slowing to a gradual stop and straightening up to neutral. Relax.

The Pendulum is particularly good for strengthening the calf and arch muscles which are used extensively in illusory techniques.

Figure 20

Figure 19

The Windmill

This is a marvellous exercise for co-ordination. Have patience and do not allow it to frustrate you.

From the neutral position, extend your arms to both sides, parallel to the floor, the muscles tensed only to the degree necessary to resist gravity, the hands completely relaxed. You are thus experiencing two widely different degrees of muscular tone: relaxed hands and tense arms (figure 21).

Leaving the left arm extended for the moment, allow the right arm to relax and drop of its own weight (figure 22). Now, as the right arm starts its swing across the body in a pendulum action (figure 23), consciously tone the arm and continue its motion in the following structured pattern. Guide the palm of the hand

Figure 21

Figure 22

Figure 23

Figure 24

across the face (figure 24), past the right ear (figure 25), behind the head (figure 26), up and diagonally out to the right side (figure 27). When the arm is again horizontal (figure 28) relax the muscle tone in order that the action can continue in an alternating pattern of relaxed, controlled, relaxed, controlled movement.

Figure 25

Figure 26

Figure 27

Figure 28

Figure 29

This exercise should be repeated with one arm and hand until it becomes automatic. Do the same with the other arm until it too is automatic. Then alternate arms as you practice. Try to establish an internal rhythm, counting one beat as the arm drops in the relaxed state, and two when the same arm extends up and out in the toned state.

When you can carry out the pattern with either arm without thought, try both arms together. On the count of two, without stopping one arm, allow the other arm to join in alternately as an after-beat. There will be continuous motion and alternating muscle tone in both arms (figures 29 to 34).

Figure 30

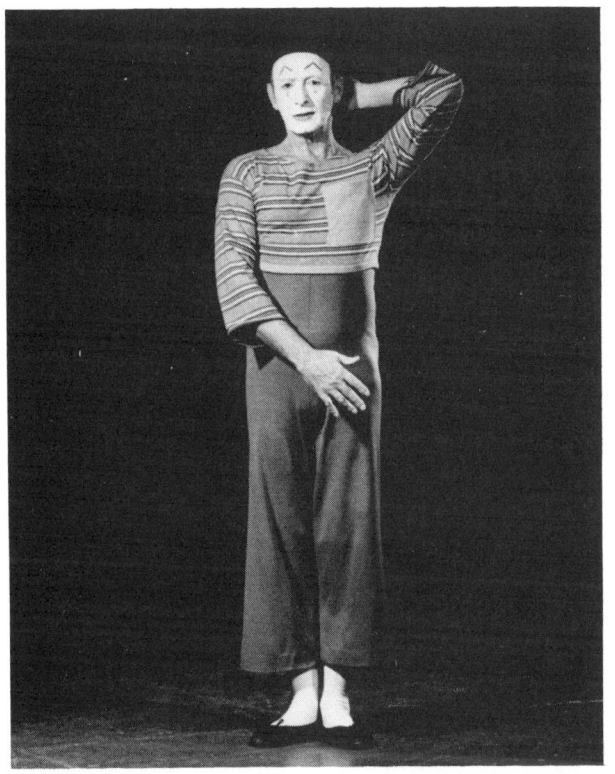

Figure 31

Figure 32

Figure 33

Figure 34

Acrobatics

Acrobatics and tumbling are good skills to acquire and in some styles of theatre, such as *Commedia dell' Arte*, they are essential.

It is not our intention to treat the subject at length here, but physical falls, faints, fights and tumbles are required in all styles of drama and the ability to accept the floor with the body in motion will, at some time, be asked of you. In order to look natural, or quite possibly unnatural, the actor must be in control at all times.

Gymnastic exercises should be done very slowly at first and, only after the achievement of complete mastery, should the pace be speeded up and the energy and dynamics strengthened. If possible, the initial work should be done on a gym mat or carpet. Only later will it be advisable to try the same work on a bare floor. In most theatres you will eventually be required to do falls on a bare stage or studio.

The Trip or Stumble

Walking at a moderate pace, place the top of the toes of the left foot against the heel of the right foot. Now try and take a step forward with the left foot. This will effectively cause you to trip over your own foot. Recover from your imbalance and look back to the spot where you tripped as if there were an object there. This all happens so quickly that the audience will quite readily accept it as a stumble.

The situation might call for you to trip and fall completely to the floor. In this case, after the self-trip, quickly bend at right angles from the waist, bend your knees and put your hands on the floor in front of you, sliding one arm out and away from you as you roll over on your back or recover in some other fashion.

Don't forget to add the actor's belief in the situation.

The Faint

Start from the neutral position with the point of levity active. Take your weight on the foot opposite the side to which you are going to fall. Move the other foot back and gently kneel on that leg to the floor.

Just as you are about to sit on the heel of the kneeling leg, shift your weight to the side on which you wish to fall and accept the floor with the side of your thigh and buttocks. Slide the upper part of your body to the floor, taking the weight on your hands and arms as they extend forward and to the side.

Practise this several times. When you can control all physical phases of the faint, add the inner feeling to the fall. Let yourself feel dizzy. Completely relax your body except for those muscles needed to control the fall. The rhythm should start slowly and become more rapid as you move closer to the floor.

A faint to the back is similar, except that you turn the knee of the kneeling leg outward from the hip joint and shift your weight backwards, at the same time rounding your back into a curve. Accept the floor with your buttocks and gently roll back onto the upper part of your body until you are supine. Be careful not to strike your head on the floor at the last moment. An arm extended to the rear and a little to one side, sliding along the floor will give more control.

The Forward Roll

Dramatically effective moments can grow out of the simple forward or backward somersault. Somersaults can mark the end of a trip or stumble or they can be part of a stage fight. In a farce or a broad theatrical style, they can be effective and uproariously funny on their own. A character, if convulsed by hysterical laughter or drowning in buckets of tears, can be plunged into a forward or backward roll.

Start from the neutral position. Take a small step forward with one foot. Bend from the waist. Place both hands on the floor in front of you about shoulder width apart and comfortably in front of your forward foot.

Lower your chin to your chest and gently fall forward, allowing the back of your head to accept the floor. At the same time, give a little push with your legs and round your back as you roll over completely. Practice several times, then increase the strength of your push until there is enough momentum to propel you over in a tucked position and carry you back up to a standing position.

When you can do the forward roll from a standing position, try approaching it from a slow walk. Without stopping, go into the roll, up onto your feet and continue the walk.

After considerable practise, try the forward roll from a run, leaping into the roll, then, quickly tucking the body and completing the roll, first in a high fashion as if leaping over a window sill, then in an elongated fashion as if leaping over several barrels in a row.

The Backward Roll

Standing in the neutral position, take a small pace backward with one foot. Bend from the waist and knees as if to sit. Allow your weight to fall backwards, your buttocks accepting the floor.

Continue the motion by tucking your chin into your chest, rounding your back and pushing your weight backwards with your legs, all the while remaining in the tucked position. As you start to roll over onto your shoulders and head, place your hands, facing behind you, on the floor at either side of your head.

Push upwards and backwards with your arms as your feet rediscover the floor and the momentum allows you to recover to the standing position.

When you can execute this roll easily, make it part of a dramatic situation. Imagine a person pushing you backwards so that, in effect, you take one or two little steps backward, do the backward roll and recover to a standing, aggressive position ready to protect yourself.

Try it also as if you were being pushed from the back. Turn quickly and do the backward roll.

Do a series of alternate forward and backward rolls as if an aggressive person is pushing you down each time you recover to a standing position.

Part II
Manipulatory Techniques

Figure 35

Accent: Dynamic: Clic: Toc

These expressions are more or less synonymous in describing that heightened moment of contrast between movement and stillness or stillness and movement. It may involve the entire body or only parts of it.

In manipulation and fixed point accent may be described as a slight surge of muscular energy which fills the hand at the precise last instant before it closes to take the space substance of an imaginary object, or the immediate draining of muscular energy at the precise instant the hand opens and relaxes to release the space substance.

Dynamic is the technique which gives the illusion of solidity and concreteness to the imaginary object created in manipulation. It also serves as punctuation in the physical phrases of silent motion, giving it accents and a dynamic, much like the rhythms in a well-read piece of prose.

The French refer to the moment as "Toc," some American mimes have coined the word "Clic," but whatever it is called, it must never be omitted from your work.

Without accent, performance is pedestrian and the moves are unclear and non-communicative. Used well, a performance takes on a vitality; the moves become precise and readable, the illusions believable. Each has an economy of its own, clean and dynamic.

The Fixed Point

Fixed point is an important technique and one which at first may be difficult to execute. The theory is quite simple to comprehend but to master, it requires practice. The success of manipulatory illusion depends, in great measure, on the perfection of fixed point technique.

A fixed point is any point in a given spatial area which does not move, except at the will of the mime (figure 35). It is usually created by the hand adopting a definite shape in stillness, suggesting the essence of the object being manipulated or used. A flat shape might suggest the surface of a wall. A round shape could suggest a ship's railing, an immovable railing attached to the ship's deck.

In both these instances the objects are relatively stationary, and the hand could, in reality, slide along or over the object. However, in mime, this cannot be done or the illusion will never be established. Take the example of the ship's railing: if the hand first slides along the rail, the illusion created is that of pushing or pulling some undefined object.

First and foremost, several fixed points or specifics must be established and manipulated on the imaginary object to define its fixedness, its position, its texture, and as many other features as can be projected.

The Baton and Variations

This is an exercise in manipulation involving a perfectly round shape of the hand. Make a circle of the fingers and the thumb. Leave a small gap between the curved index finger and the thumb. You have created the rounded space substance of the imaginary object, in this case a baton with the hand closed upon it.

Our imaginary baton is a little larger than the popular twirling baton, approximately five centimetres in diameter and about one metre in length. It is polished and smooth as it is made of a hard wood, a piece of oak dowling.

Principle: Hands must open to receive the object and must open to let go of an object.

Bend down and pick up the imaginary baton which is lying on the floor at your feet. Grasp it with both hands, about shoulder width apart, and lift it in a realistic fashion to a position in front of you (figure 36). Visualize a short length of baton protruding to the left of your left hand and a similar short piece to the right of your right hand.

Both of these hand attitudes are termed "fixed points," although they will move in space at your volition and always relative to each other. They are fixed and held equidistant by the imaginary substance of the baton between your hands, regardless of the spatial plane into which the arms will carry them, vertical, horizontal, oblique or random.

The object of the exercise is to rotate the baton on a fixed imaginary axis from a horizontal to a vertical position and back to the horizontal.

Having picked up the baton, the backs of both hands are now facing the ceiling.

Take the right hand off the baton by immediately opening and relaxing the muscle tone and unshaping the hand: that is, make the hand into any shape other than the round shape described before.

Continue with the right hand and grasp the baton again, in exactly the same place, but this time with the hand turned upside down, its back facing the floor (figure 37).

Figure 36

Figure 37

Now, rotate the baton counter-clockwise on its imaginary axis so that it is vertical and the right hand is directly above the left hand (figure 38).

Figure 38

Again open the right hand, relax and unshape it immediately, and grasp that piece of the imaginary baton which is below the left hand, still keeping the baton vertical (figure 39).

Release the left hand by opening, relaxing and unshaping, and raise it, turning the hand upside down, thumb down, and grasping the imaginary baton from the inside at a point in front of the forehead (figure 40).

Figure 39

Figure 40

Now rotate the baton in the same direction as before, this time from the vertical to the horizontal (figure 41).

Figure 41

The hands should be back in the starting position, with the slight exception that the right hand will now be slightly further to the right on what has been the short extension of the imaginary baton.

Each time the baton is grasped or released, there should be the accompanying accent or clic. Continue to rotate the baton around and around its imaginary axis, occasionally changing directions.

Baton Variation: The Plus Sign

For variation, change the imagery from the single baton to a plus sign with a fixed axis at its centre. Rotate the horizontal member so that the imaginary member which has been vertical, becomes horizontal. Establish the new horizontal member by placing the hands on it and rotate again to the vertical.

Repeat over and over, experimenting to find the most economical and comfortable manner of accomplishing this simple exercise.

Baton Variation: The Multiplication Sign

Change the imaginary object to a cross or multiplication sign. The object of the exercise is to rotate one of the oblique members top to bottom and then the other in the same fashion.

In the foregoing exercises, you may measure your accuracy by gauging the position of the imaginary object in relation to the lines created by the real objects in the room: horizontal ceiling, floor and furniture lines; the vertical, oblique or random lines of corners, picture frames, windows or doors.

Adjust and correct each time you observe a difference in angle or level, and also check and adjust for the imaginary plane in which you are manipulating the imaginary object.

Analyse the muscular feeling when your hands are placed and shaped correctly, and try to develop the muscle memory mentioned in another chapter.

The Fireman's Pole

This exercise will develop the idea of fixed point. Imagine a fireman's pole, about twelve centimetres in diameter, and made of metal. The top is firmly attached to the ceiling and the bottom fixed to the floor.

The exercise is simply to walk past the pole, reaching for it at shoulder height, grasping it firmly in the hand as you pass, and then allowing it to pull you to a halt before you release the hand.

The hand must not move either horizontally or vertically or slide around the pole. The wrist is free to move in a limited fashion and, of course, the rest of the arm responds as you pass the pole.

Now let us analyse the exercise in more detail.

Walk casually. It is impossible to control the fixed point if the walk is too fast. About two paces before you reach the pole, extend your arm fully in front of you towards the imaginary object. The hand should be open, the wrist in an extended vertical position: the forearm and upper arm, including the shoulder, should also be fully extended, reaching for the imaginary pole.

At this point, grasp the pole with your hand, allowing for its diameter, with a marked accent or dynamic as the hand closes around it.

Continue to walk past and, as the wrist bends in the direction of the walk, immediately contract the arm muscles involved until it is necessary to elongate them again as you are pulled to a stop. You are now free to open your hand and release the pole.

Try the same exercise using the other hand to grasp the pole.

Some identifiable mark on the floor should be used for the location of the imaginary pole so you will be able to gauge how well you have kept the fixed point in position.

Another way to practice when working in groups is to pair off and have one partner simulate the pole by bending the elbow and holding the forearm vertical and rigid, to the side. The practicing partner uses this forearm a few times to get a realistic feeling of the pole.

He then grasps an imaginary pole close to the partner's forearm, using the arm now only to see how well he has maintained the fixed point. Both of you can see how well you are progressing. Practice several times, then reverse roles.

The Slalom

This is a group exercise, still with fixed point as its main objective, but which also embraces concentration and focus.

The exercise progresses from pole to pole, one actor following another, pausing just long enough to allow the person behind to take the pole ahead and release the pole behind.

Imagine a row of several slalom flags in a straight line about one metre apart. The leader of the group starts off — as in the fireman's pole — slightly to the left of the imaginary line of poles. As the leader passes the first pole, and before releasing his right hand, he takes the second pole in his left hand and waits until number two of the group has taken the first pole in his right hand.

The leader then releases his right hand and, keeping his left hand at its fixed point, walks between the first and second poles. He goes around the second pole and takes the third pole in his right hand. Again he waits for number two, who follows, and, in turn, waits for number three to grasp the first pole before he releases his hand.

The slalom requires a good deal of practice at a slow rhythm, as well as sensitivity, awareness, and co-operation. Be prepared for utter chaos at first! But sooner or later everyone will understand and achieve the essential unity. Start with small groups, enlarging them and changing leaders often.

The Wall

We have stressed the importance of fixed point in manipulation and the creation of illusion: "making visible the invisible," as one great mime so aptly phrased it. Let us continue to stress this aspect of manipulation as we examine in detail an exercise in which the hand is flat, as opposed to round or any intermediate position.

As always, start from the neutral position with the point of levity active, in a relaxed, comfortable and vertical stance. Loosely shake out the hands to insure that they will be relaxed and comparatively unshaped.

With the "actor's belief," as opposed to the actual belief of realism, focus on an imaginary wall about half a metre in front of you. Try to find an inner state that will allow you to imaginatively "see" the wall. The more honest and believable the mental, emotional, and physical states of the performer, the stronger the "actor's belief" will be in the reality of the situation.

We will begin by establishing a rectangular pattern using one hand to define the fixed point. Gently bring the arm up and sharply place the hand flat on the imaginary wall. The clic should occur at the very last moment and the dynamic tone of the hand should be sustained as you imaginatively feel the resistance of the wall.

Analyse the attitude of the hand. The palm and fingers must be straight and flat in order to project the essence of the wall. Avoid too much tone or the pulpy part of the palm will create an undulated "S" shape; avoid understated tone or there will be a concave attitude in the hand which will also reduce the illusion of a flat surface.

The hand must be absolutely perpendicular. This is controlled by the angle of the wrist, which will always be ninety degrees or greater, and the placement of the hand, high or low on the wall.

There is selectivity and freedom of choice in the execution of these manoeuvres. Logic also plays a great part, and you will find, for instance, that it may be necessary at times to bend the knees or stand on the toes in order to execute the illusion.

The first principle of fixed point is that once it has been established, it must not be erased or dissipated unless the action requires it. Therefore, sustain the fixed point with the first hand, while the other hand is creating a second fixed point. Gently bring the arm up and, with a clic, place the second hand fixed point a shoulder width away from the first hand but on the same plane (figure 42).

This suggests width. The first fixed point may now be erased or dissipated. This is accomplished by relaxing and immediately removing and unshaping the first hand, then, gently placing it, with the clic, at a point above and diagonal to the second hand which is still sustaining its muscular tone. This third point establishes the suggestion of height.

Figure 42

Figure 43

Now the second hand relaxes and is immediately taken off the wall and placed at an imaginary spot above, and opposite to the other hand and on the same plane. In effect, a small rectangle has been created, imaginatively suggesting width and height and effectively creating the illusion of a flat surface immediately in front of you.

This sequence should be repeated several times; stand in the same spot, then kneel, to create multiple rectangular phrases.

Now you are ready to enlarge your wallscape by suggesting further dimensions to the left or right of where you stand, by moving along the wall.

Again, simple logic will help in planning your actions. For instance, if you create a flat fixed point with your right hand, and then attempt to sustain that point while moving to your right, you will almost immediately find that you are walking into your own right arm and that the effect is minimal.

Therefore, create a fixed point with your right hand directly in front of you. Sustaining that point, allow the tendons and muscles to elongate as you move to the left of that point a step or two. Do not allow the fixed point to move.

Now create a fixed point with the left hand, a step or two to your left. Free the right hand and, as you continue to move left, quickly use the right hand to create a third point just above and adjacent to the left hand, immediately freeing the left hand before you find yourself walking into your left arm.

Continue in one direction for several paces, then reverse your direction and the pattern of fixed points. Be aware that this is primarily an exercise. To execute the number of fixed points suggested here in performance would be an over-statement. In a later chapter we will discuss economy and selectivity at greater length.

So far we have only established width and height in general terms. Now we may complete the illusion.

In order to show the end of the wall, make the hand into a right angle, with a clic, by bending the fingers straight from the large knuckles, fingers together and thumb unnoticeable, melded against the index big knuckle. Create first one fixed point at the end of your wall and then a second, vertically above the first one, suggesting a right-angled corner of undefined thickness (figure 43).

Now, release the bottom fixed point and walk around the end of the wall, releasing the top fixed point as you move away from the illusion you have established.

Similarly, to define the top of the wall, create two fixed points in a line horizontal to the forehead, the hands in the same right-angular shape (figure 44). The illusion can be heightened by rising onto your toes as you attempt to look over the wall (figure 45).

Figure 44

Each time you create a fixed point or dissipate one, remember to give the dynamic or clic. Be very careful when establishing the height of the wall not to pull the wall down into the floor as you go up onto your toes. Your hands must maintain the fixed point on the top of the wall.

Experiment with other imagery to delineate a variety of flat planes: a table top, desk, work bench, short order grill, whatever you may need to tell your story.

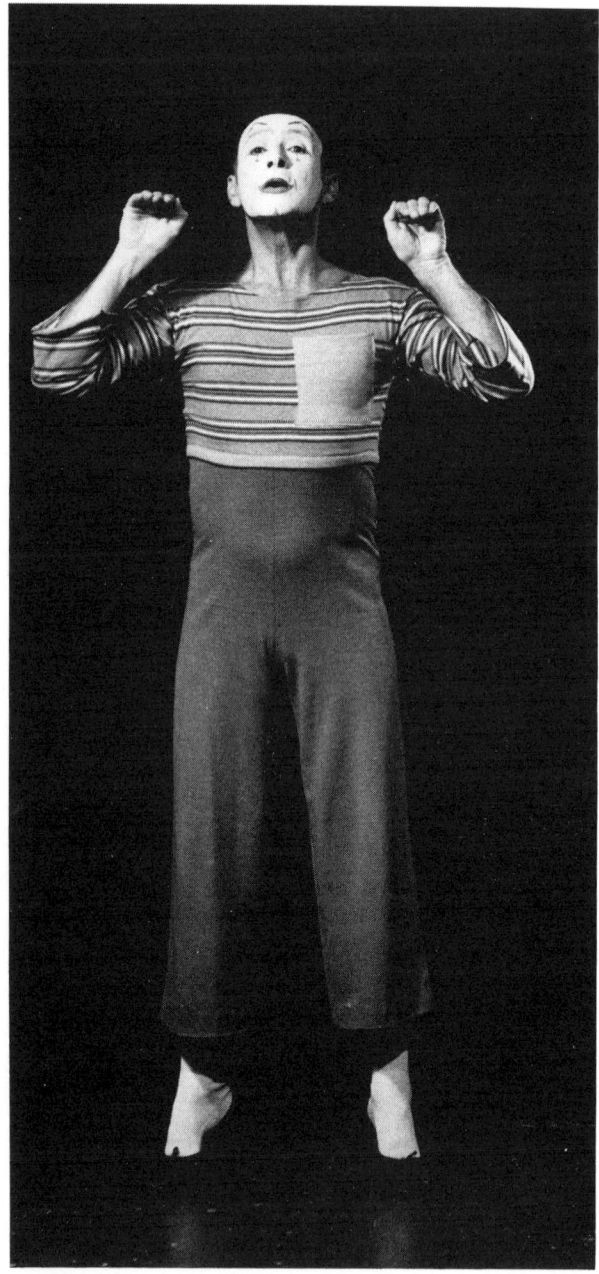

Figure 45

The Building Brick

This is a more complex manipulation than the baton or the wall, in that it involves demonstrating more than two dimensions. It is excellent for improving the coordination and flexibility of the hands.

Imagine an ordinary rectangular building brick. The object of the exercise is to manipulate the brick from the ends, turning it over away from you, each time adjusting the hand attitudes to the narrower and broader thicknesses of the widths.

In other words the wide plane of the image (the brick, here) will progress from facing the ceiling, to the audience in front, to the floor, to you yourself and back to the ceiling again as you continue the manipulation.

To make the rectangular shapes and the widest width that will be required of the hands, first try to form the best right angle that you can between the fingers, bent at the second or middle knuckles, and the palm of the hand. The bottom right angle is created by the palm of the hand and the thumb extended out parallel to the floor.

For the smaller thickness, create a right angle from the large knuckles of the hand, and the fingers straight and extended parallel to the floor. The thumb will complete the third side of the rectangle, also extended parallel to the floor.

Pick the brick up by its wider width, both hands in the wide U-shaped attitude, fixed points the length of the brick apart. Hold it in front of you, the wider plane facing your face (figure 46).

Rotate the brick away from you, both hands turning simultaneously (figure 47). Release the left hand fixed point and turn it back to take the brick by its narrower thickness (figure 48). Do the same with the right hand. Rotate it away from you again and continue the exercise by grasping the wider width of the brick as above (figure 49).

This exercise can be modified to indicate any small three dimensional object. Try a match box or packet of cigarettes.

Figure 46

Figure 47

Figure 48

Figure 49

Economy and Selectivity

When you have mastered the techniques in the foregoing manipulation exercises, try to be very selective and economical in the number of specific movements you choose to create them.

For example, in creating the illusion of a wall, think of the proscenium arch of the stage as an artist's canvas. Your wallscape is to be a painting using as few brush strokes as possible.

Using your hands as the brushes, start from one side of the area and, with your actor's belief, "see" the wall. Establish a fixed point and travel two steps, establishing two further fixed points. Take two more steps just looking at the wall, with your arms relaxed at your sides. Establish the top of the wall and attempt to look over it. Release the fixed points and walk another two steps, again just looking at your wall. Place one more fixed point, establish the end and walk away. You have created the illusion.

The audience will be quite content with the number of specifics you have shown them and will accept the reality of the illusion, provided you do. This economy of motion serves to clarify, whereas too many movements become either boring or unclear in their repetition.

Do not be confused, however, between performance and practice in class. Repetition of the exercises for technique, much like practicing musical scales over and over, is vital.

Muscle Memory

An important side benefit of practicing these exercises and techniques regularly is the development of what can best be described as muscle memory. After a time you will find that the muscles involved begin to respond to your every thought and feeling, without your being conscious of that effort.

As you are executing a particular technique, analyse the muscular feeling, correcting the technique if necessary: try to find that same feeling on the next repetition. Memorizing and achieving the muscle feeling is part of memorizing and perfecting the technique.

In the exercise of the wall for example, fill the hand with energy; correct and adjust the flat appearance until it is as perfectly flat as possible. Note the feeling, then relax the muscles and unshape the hand, repeating this each time you practice. Eventually the hand will respond without conscious effort on your part.

As each of the specific hand and body attitudes covered in this text becomes part of your muscle memory, you will discover your repertoire rapidly expanding. Many moves are similar and learning new ones becomes a matter of adjustment and, of course, belief in the imagery of that move.

This last aspect, belief, should be emphasized. Efficient technical execution is not enough in itself. The proper inner state, your emotional involvement and your precise analysis of the imaginary object or situation, is essential at all times. Without this enrichment, the execution will be shallow, cold and clinical.

PART III
Illusory Techniques

Walking in Place: Front View

Start from the neutral position with the point of levity active, feet slightly apart and parallel to each other.

Take the full weight on the left foot and raise the heel of the right foot until just the ball of the foot is on the floor, with the heel almost at right angles to the floor (figure 50).

Figure 50

Shift the weight onto the ball of the right foot for a brief instant and then flatten the foot

so there is a full-footed base. At the same time take the left foot back, close to the floor and parallel to it, a short pace (figure 51); then,

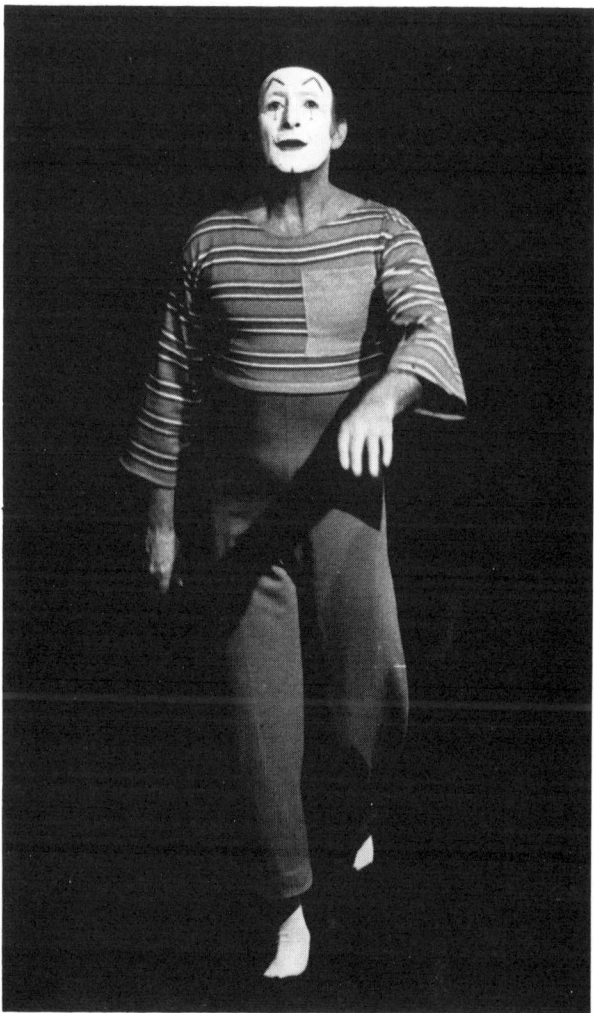

Figure 51

bending the knee slightly, bring the foot quickly forward again onto the ball of the foot, toe to toe with the right foot, feet just slightly apart (figure 52).

For the purpose of analysis, pause in this position. You will notice that your feet are exactly opposite to the first position.

Now repeat this physical phrase in the opposite manner, and once again pause (figures 53, 54 and 55). You have completed two steps "walking in place." Repeat a few times so that the feet are reacting easily, there is no balance problem, and the body is not bouncing up and down.

Figure 52   **Figure 53**   **Figure 54**   **Figure 55**

If this latter is happening, you are going up onto the ball of the foot that is acting as the base, or you are straightening that leg before the foot starts to flatten rather than as the foot is flattening. Try to lead with the knee and

draw the heel of that foot off the floor; the distance that the knee goes forward compensates for the height the heel is drawn off the floor, with the result that the rest of the body remains still.

Figure 56

Figure 57

Figure 58

Now add your arms to the illusion. They should swing naturally and not be held in a prancing position. Starting as before with your weight on the left foot, swing and stretch the right arm out in front of you about waist high at the fullest height of the swing (figure 56).

At the same time that you exchange the position of the feet, exchange the position of the arms (figure 57). Initially it is wise to pause after each phrase of execution at the point where the feet are toe to toe.

When hands and feet are well co-ordinated, strive to take the pause out of the illusion and have one phrase follow the other immediately (figures 58 and 59).

Figure 59   Figure 60

These are the cold mechanics of the illusion and by themselves are not sufficient, except as an exercise. You must now consider the inner state, the actor's belief in the situation that requires the function of walking.

Walking in Place: Side view

From the neutral position with the feet just

slightly apart, as in the front view, take the weight of the body on the full flat of the right foot.

Place the left foot forward as if taking a short step, keeping it parallel to the floor (figure 60). Immediately draw it back toe to toe with the right foot, transferring the weight of the body onto it.

At the same time that you draw the left foot back, bend the right knee forward and draw the right heel off the floor so that you are on the ball of the foot with the heel almost at right angles to the floor (figure 61). At this point pause for purposes of control and analysis.

Now repeat this phrase using opposite feet and pause once again (figure 62). Practice this walking motion over and over until control is perfect, and the body is not bouncing up and down.

The purpose of this technique is to give an illusion of the body moving through space. As you draw the foot back, lead with the heel so that the stronger impulse (what you as the actor believe) is of each foot being drawn back and not of the feet kicking forward.

When the foot movements are fluent, add your arms to complete the illusion. The arrival of the right hand at its fullest height, waist high, should synchronize with the arrival of the left foot at its highest position, as it is drawn onto the ball, and vice versa.

As before, when the pauses are no longer needed, abandon them. The actor's belief will complete the illusion.

Figure 61

Figure 62

Walking up Stairs

The technique of walking in place, front view, lends itself well to the creation of other illusions.

In order to create the impression of walking up stairs, add an imaginary hand rail that starts a little lower than shoulder height and at a full arm's length in front of the body, to one side or the other. The imaginary rail, then, cuts your body at hip height and descends lower behind you.

Whereas while walking-in-place you were cautioned not to rise onto the ball of the foot, in walking up stairs it is necessary to rise for an initial brief instance, and, then, quickly accept the floor with the flat of the foot.

Specifically, place the imaginary rail on your right side. Take the weight of your body on the left foot (figure 63). Leading with the knee, lift the heel of the right foot off the floor, briefly rising onto the ball and then quickly accepting the floor flat-footed (figure 64). At the same time reach forward and grasp the imaginary railing at shoulder height and draw it down in an oblique straight line to a point just past your right hip.

As you are accepting the floor with your right foot flat, take a vertical step in place with the left foot, ending on the ball (figure 65). Pause for control and analysis.

Figure 63   **Figure 64**   **Figure 65**

Now shift the weight onto the ball of the left foot (figure 66), and quickly accept the floor. Step in place, this time with the right foot, once again rising onto the ball of the foot (figure 67). At the same time move the right arm up, and then down and along the imaginary stair railing. The hand on the railing should start its downward motion at the same moment you rise onto the ball of the foot, and complete its motion as the same foot becomes flat. A variation on the use of the railing is to halve the distance the hand travels and take another pace before the complete distance is used.

This illusion may be performed in place, or the body may travel laterally by allowing one toe to move a few inches in front of the other each time.

Strive for a realistic impression of going up stairs by giving a sharp accent on the rising motions and a softer feeling as the foot becomes flat and the arm slides down along the railing. The illusion may be strengthened by looking up at an oblique angle before taking the first step, and by looking down over the railing after taking five or six steps.

Figure 66

Walking Down Stairs

This technique is similar to walking up stairs, except that this time the railing rises from a point in front of you at waist level to a point at chest level. Draw your hand up the oblique line of the rail, releasing the fixed point as it passes behind the chest.

In this downward illusion you do not rise onto the ball of the foot, but accent the downward motions as the foot becomes flat on the stair. As always, the actor's belief must give truth to the illusion.

Figure 67

Walking against the Wind

Once the technique of walking in place, front view, is mastered, many environmental colours may be added. In essence, it becomes an actor's problem to add those shadow moves which are more a result of belief than of technique.

You can convince an audience that you are walking through water, or through mud, or leaves, simply by responding physically to your belief in the situation. The stronger you build this actor's belief internally and the more you allow the intuitive shadow moves to respond, the more readily the audience will accept the illusion and become involved with the situation on stage.

For example, in walking against the wind, you might begin by walking in place, front view, enjoying a beautiful day. Allow your imagination to feel the first gust of wind. There may be no physical response to it, but there certainly would be an internal one.

Several more gusts strengthen this feeling and your steps might begin to falter as their intensity increases. Gale winds might severely slow your pace to the point where a mighty push against the wind with your entire body leaning forward would become necessary. You hunch your shoulders, pull your coat together and turn your back to the wind. A particularly strong gust blows you back or to the side, a step or more.

Remember, it is better to do too little than too much — be honest and economical in your responses.

Figure 68

Figure 69

Running: in Place

Start from the neutral position with the point of levity active. Even when you are instructed below to bend forward from the waist, keep the point of levity working.

Take the weight of the body on the left foot, and bend forward at a thirty degree angle. At the same time, bend the right leg at the knee, raising it from the hip until the top of the leg is parallel to the floor.

Simultaneously, bend the right arm at the elbow. Take the arm back from the shoulder until the elbow is above the line of your back. Bend the left arm and raise it to the front at the same time as the right arm goes back. Your left leg is for the moment straight and is the base upon which you are balancing (figure 68).

We now add another dimension: a small ''jig'' executed by the left foot and leg. As the knee of the right leg straightens on the one count, the knee of the left leg goes forward and back, simply drawing the heel off the floor and quickly returning it to the floor (refer back to figure 69). Do not rise onto the ball of the foot.

This little ''jig'' tends to suggest that the balancing leg is also in an attitude of running. The torso remains in a fixed position throughout the illusion with minimal up and down movement. The illusion is most effective when done with the upstage leg executing the jig. Remember that the actor's belief is fundamental to all illusory techniques!

The right leg now describes the following sequence of four beats:

Count one: lower the right foot to brush the floor opposite the ankle of the left foot, not in front of it (figures 69 and 70).
Count two: straighten the right leg as you extend it behind you and lift the foot knee-high off the floor (figures 71 and 72).
Count three: sustain this position, bending the knee fully (figure 73).

Figure 70   **Figure 71**

Count four: bring the leg, still bent, forward from the hip until it again reaches the starting position (figure 74).

At the same time, the following two movements are also taking place: As the knee of the right leg straightens on the downward move, on count one, move the right arm (which is akimbo and to the back) forward and, on the second count, extend it to the front just as the right leg extends fully to the rear.

You will observe now that the earlier description of the movement of the right arm occurs on counts three and four of the leg sequence. Repeat the sequence over and over several times to co-ordinate the right leg and the arms until there is a comfortable flow of movement.

Figure 72

Figure 73

Figure 74

Running: Mobile

The illusion of running may be executed in place, or may incorporate movement, if required. It grows out of the technique of walking in place, front view.

Start from the neutral position and begin to walk in place, front view. After taking a few steps, imagine that a bus you were hoping to catch is already at the stop, half a city block in front of you.

Quicken your pace and begin to lean forward from the hips (figure 75) allowing your legs to rise higher and higher off the floor (figures 76 and 77) behind you. At the same time reach a little farther forward with your arms in order to compensate. As the bus starts to move, increase the rhythm until you are literally sprinting.

The bus picks up speed and you realize you cannot possibly catch it. Reverse the rhythm and slowly return to a walk.

At the height of the run you will notice that you are simply exchanging foot positions, from the ball of one foot to the ball of the other, as each leg leaves the floor and returns to it. The body leans forward at an extended angle and the torso moves only minimally; arms and legs create the illusion of running through space.

As in the walk, this illusion can be made slightly mobile by allowing the toe of one foot to advance slightly in front of the other each time it returns to the floor.

Figure 75   **Figure 76**   **Figure 77**

Skating: in Place

Start from the neutral position, and be aware of the point of levity. With the weight on the right foot, bend forward about thirty degrees. Push the left foot obliquely back and to the side, at about a forty-five degree angle to the line of direction. At the same time, extend the left arm to the front and the right arm to the back (figure 78).

Continue by dragging the left foot back (across the imaginary ice) into the line of direction (figure 79) and then forward until it is in line with the right foot, toe to toe. With a quick little exchange, transfer the weight from the right foot onto the left.

Now, repeat with the right foot sliding back and to the side on an oblique angle, then into the line of direction and forward toe to toe. Make the quick exchange of weight from left to right. The arms also exchange positions (figure 80).

Figure 78

Figure 79

Figure 80

This is primarily a static illusion, but it may be made to move in similar fashion to the other illusions that shift the balance from one leg to the other. It is only in those illusions where the balance is at all times on one leg that mobility is limited or impossible.

Do not forget your actor's belief.

Skating: Mobile

From the neutral position, bend slightly forward and, with your left foot, push yourself to your right, left arm extended to your front, right arm behind you. The right foot executes the little shuffle pattern described immediately below.

The shuffle pattern is accomplished in this instance by taking the balance from the toe to the heel, to the toe to the heel repeating in rapid sequence from one to the other. As the balance is on the heel, pivot the toe to the right, then quickly shift the balance to the toe and pivot the heel slightly to the right. This will move you a short distance to your right.

Now, quickly shift your weight to your left foot by pushing off with the right. Repeat the shuffle, this time on the left foot, and move a short distance to your left. Maintain your balance by moving your arms just as if you were skating.

Repeat the above, moving alternately from side to side a number of times. Simulate racing in competition or pleasure skating with the more leisurely classic attitude of hands clasped behind the back.

Figure 81

The Gondolier: in Place

Imagine yourself a gondolier, standing at the stern of the gondola on the rear part of the gunwale where it joins to form a small platform deck.

You have a pole some four metres long, sufficient to reach the bottom of the canal, usually a metre or so deep, leaving enough of the pole comfortably above the water line, so that you can manipulate it. Here are the simple mechanics of poling a boat through a shallow body of water.

Stand in the neutral position, facing mostly to the port or left-hand side of the boat, feet slightly apart, the left foot pointing left, the right foot facing front toward the bow of the boat.

Place the hands approximately shoulder-width apart on the middle section of the pole. With both hands, the palm of the right and the back of the left facing the body, lift the long pole which is lying across the gunwale at your feet.

Raise the pole to a position over your head where you can plunge it down in vertical fashion in front of your right foot and into the water (figure 81).

When your hands are approximately opposite your chest, release the left hand, fixed point, continuing to thrust the pole down with the right hand (figure 82), taking a new fixed point with the left hand about half a metre above the right, in hand-over-hand fashion (figure 83).

Figure 82

Figure 83

Figure 84   Figure 85   Figure 86

Immediately release the right hand as the left continues its downward thrust, and take another fixed point with the right hand on the imaginary extension of the pole (figure 84). The hands, in addition to thrusting the pole downwards, travel at the same time across the plane of the body from right to left, or front to rear (figure 85).

As the pole travels down and across your body, the angle of the pole changes from the vertical to an oblique forty-five degrees until the end of the manoeuvre, when the right hand gives a final push on the end of the pole (figure 86), actually against the last left hand fixed point. You can put hand against hand (figure 87).

The last left hand fixed point begins the retrieve, which is accomplished in similar hand-over-hand fashion. This time the pole is kept at an angle of forty-five degrees (figure 88), until it has cleared the resistance of the imaginary water. When your hands have returned to what is approximately the middle of the imaginary pole (figure 89), you are free to start the second stroke. Lift the pole over your head and again plunge it vertically into the water, again past the right foot (figure 90).

The body should be free to face a little ahead or behind and to reach and bend as the movement requires. In addition to the mechanics described, you must remember to include the inner state. You must "believe" in the imaginary reality of the pole, the sleek gondola, and the effort needed to push the gondola through the imaginary buoyant water. Acting is believing!

Figure 87

Figure 88

Figure 89

Figure 90

The Gondolier: Mobile

The boat, whether it be a gondola or skiff or other craft, can be made to move across the stage. If you have ever seen the beautiful *Legend of the White Serpent* performed by the Peking Opera Company, you will remember how wonderfully effective this illusion can be when competently performed.

In this mime the princess and her lady-in-waiting are fleeing from a wicked war lord when they come to a river. An old ferryman takes them across to safety. As they get into the imaginary craft, the trio immediately suggests the liquidity of the water with subtle undulations. Then as the boatman poles them across, the three move in concert laterally across the stage, the handmaiden gently brushing her lady's hair. It is a beautifully theatrical scene.

The poling action of the boatman is performed exactly as described earlier. The lateral movement is accomplished by the double shuffle of the feet. The performer is costumed so that the mechanics of the feet may not be apparent.

The double shuffle is accomplished by standing with the feet a bit apart. Lift the toe of the left foot and, at the same time, lift the heel of the right foot, simultaneously pivoting each foot on its respective toe or heel. Now repeat the movement, this time lifting the heel of the left foot and the toe of the right and again pivoting to the right. Continue in a rapid and controlled manner, so that a very smooth continuous movement carries the body in a straight line to your right side.

The boatman co-ordinates this technique with that of poling the water craft, moving slowly as he overcomes the resistance of the water and speeding up as the craft poles more easily.

Passengers relate closely to the rhythms of the boatman and, perhaps, draw attention from the actual technique of combing hair, polishing a weapon, or some other simple activity.

The liquidity of the water is conveyed by the actor's belief in the situation, a slight undulation achieved by gently flexing the knees, a sense of imbalance and the resulting shadow moves.

The Canoe

In most of the illusions described, there is no absolutely definitive way in which they must be performed. It will always be a matter of choice and variation by the actor. Experience, knowledge and exposure to the realities of the techniques and of the stage will influence you.

It is a good idea to double check the actual function of real objects and their mechanisms. There are some real functions which do not transfer to the imaginary illusion of mime. For example, in reality, the hand may slide up or down a pole, a paddle, or a baton, but in mime, this action would destroy the illusion of solidity, and make it appear as if the object was being stretched.

The Canadian canoe is the craft we have in mind but, with slight modification, you could explore on your own the illusion of an outrigger canoe, or a kayak.

If you favour your right side, kneel on your right knee (figure 91). Your right hand will act as the fulcrum. It is placed fixed point and mid-distance at the throat of the paddle. The left hand is placed at the top of the paddle and acts along with the arm muscles and the body as lever power. The hands are about a metre apart and react to each other in unison, at a fixed distance from each other.

Bend from the waist, reach forward and dip the blade of the paddle down into the water (figure 92). With the arms well extended, pull the whole body back in this attitude to a vertical position (figures 93 and 94).

Figure 91

Figure 92

Figure 93

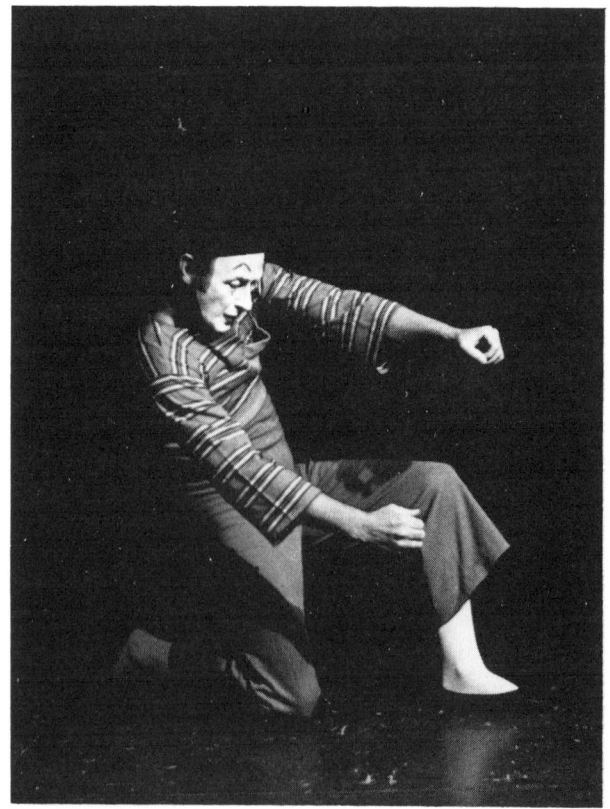

Figure 94

Figure 95

Figure 96

Figure 97

At this point, pulse the body slightly forward in a countermove as you bend the elbows and continue to pull the paddle past your left side with your arm muscles (figure 95). The right hand will pull a greater distance than the left. The paddle will now be at an angle behind you. At this point, turn the hands, turning the blade of the paddle so that its plane cuts the water. With a short stroke of the left hand, execute a little ''J'' stroke (figure 96). This stroke is used to control the direction of the bow of the canoe, much like a rudder, and to lessen the number of times one is rquired to change the paddling side. Repeat the sequence from the beginning several times, modifying the rhythms and force of the strokes. You may kneel upright or sit on your back foot; paddle to win a race or gently drift on the northern lake (figures 97 and 98). The mechanics of canoeing are rather simple. It is the craft of the actor, that will set the scene for us.

Figure 98

The Skulling Shell

From watching the Olympics or other water sports, you may have some knowledge of the mechanics of these shallow-draft boats with their seats which travel back and forth along tracks in the bottom of the craft. Their size varies from single-man and double-man to larger teams in a boat. The excitement is considerable, particularly in the larger boats as the coxswain shouts the rhythm through his megaphone, and the stroke gets faster and faster as they near the finish line.

The mechanics of the technique to be described below can be easily modified to create an illusion of any type of rowing craft. This illusion is also another example of the fact that some realistic functions cannot be emulated in mime. However, there is usually some way to suggest the illusion so that it will be accepted within the conventions of the theatre.

Sit on the floor as if you were on the movable seat of the skulling shell: body bent forward, knees drawn up to the chest between the arms, heels together and braced against an imaginary footstop on the bottom of the craft, toes in the air.

Both arms should be stretched out in front of you parallel to the floor, the hands fixed point, in baton attitude, shoulder width apart as they grasp the handles of the imaginary oars. The backs of the hands are slightly slanted to each side towards the water, suggesting the angle of the oars which are also slanted towards the water, the blades behind you.

The oarlocks are fixed at a fulcrum point at the ends of two cantilevered metal braces that extend to the left and right sides of the shell, a little in front of you, out over the water. Thus you are poised ready for the starting gun to sound.

Dip the imaginary oars down into the water by counterraising the hands slightly, at the same time pulling back with the body, arms extended, until you are leaning slightly behind an imaginary vertical line. Bend your elbows. Continue pulling the imaginary oars back with your arms until your hands are at your chest and at the same time pull your body slightly forward to the vertical position. During this manoeuvre, straighten your knees until your legs are extended straight in front of you.

Now lower your hands a little. This, in effect, raises the blades of the oars till they just clear the water at your sides and slightly in front of you. Don't forget that the boat is travelling in the direction that your back is facing.

Now twist your wrists and hands backward. This turns the blade of the oar so that it is flat on the surface of the water. Bring the oars back to the starting position, feathering the blades over the surface of the water, by pushing your hands forward and leaning forward as you draw your knees back up to your chest; your arms are once again fully extended as at the start. With a short forward turn of the hands and wrists, you are ready to begin another stroke.

In analysis, you may observe that the hands are describing an elongated oval pattern accented at each point of the oval: one away from you with a forward flick of the wrist to start the stroke; one close to you with a backward flick of the wrists to feather the blades. When you start to pull your body back to the vertical position there should be an impulse of added effort as you engage the arm muscles. Instead of the mechanized seat moving as you push against a fixed object with your feet, you are establishing quite an acceptable illusion by fixing the position of the seat and moving your feet.

The Bicycle: Unicycle

This illusion is popular and most often gets a chuckle. It is very demanding of the leg muscles and in the beginning it should not be practiced for too long a period.

The illusion of getting onto the bicycle is established in a series of important moves. Face the imaginary bicycle so that you will be mounting from the left side. Its front end is to your left.

Establish with your left hand the near grip of the handlebars (the baton) with a fixed point a little to the front of your right thigh, in line with the left hand (figure 99).

For a moment take your weight on the right foot as you place the left foot on the floor in front of you directly underneath the right hand fixed point (figure 100). This foot move is extremely important as it will be the base upon which you will stand and the centre of gravity after the next move.

Now, removing the right hand fixed point from the seat, reach over for the other handlebar grip. At the same time lift the right foot, in the case of a ladies bicycle which has no bar, through the open V-like part of the bicycle. Place it immediately next to the left foot while you sit on the seat with a little wiggle of your posterior to suggest that you are firmly seated. In the case of a man's bicycle, which has the

diamond frame, the right leg is raised to straddle the seat and brought down beside the left foot.

When your balance is secure, place both hands firmly in fixed point on the handlebars, lift the right foot and place it on the pedal about knee high (figure 101).

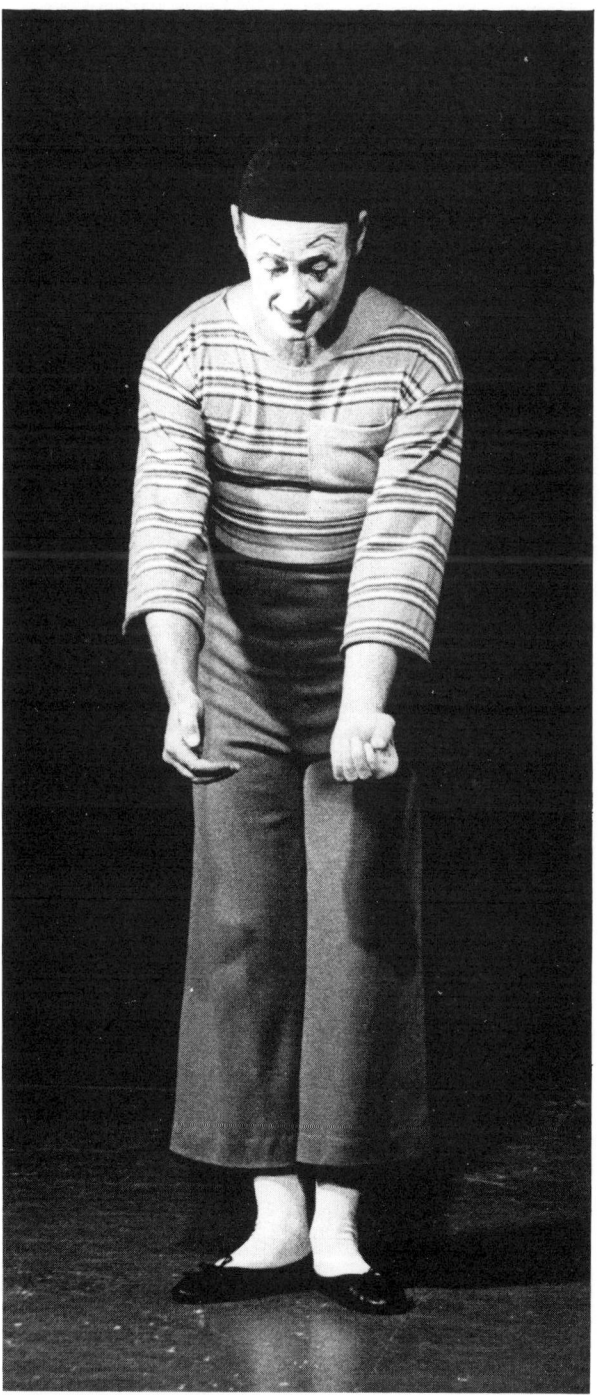

Figure 99

Figure 100

Figure 101

Figure 102

The right foot then describes a circle around an imaginary axis just above the left ankle. This is a very minimal move. The heel should not go much beyond the shank of the left foreleg (figure 102). The lower extremity of the circle is governed by the floor (figure 103) and the rear perimeter is about correct if the toe is not much past the calf of the left leg (figure 104).

Figure 103

Figure 104

Figure 105

As the right foot is describing the action of the pedal, the left knee bends and draws the heel of the left foot off the floor and immediately returns it to the floor. This move is similar to the "jig" move executed in "Running in Place: Static."

You are, in fact, balancing for a split-second on the ball of the left foot without actually rising

up on to it. This move should be executed as the foot of the right leg is approaching the floor. The knees should be working in opposite directions.

A very funny effect can be realized if, with control, you synchronize the knee motions so that they are both going forward at the same time. This makes the body rise and fall as if the bicycle hit a bump or had a flat in the tire. You might glance back at the rear tire, react — and tumble head over heels!

The illusion of a unicycle can be simply done by straddling the seat (figure 105), starting the pedal mechanics (figure 106), and using the arms in a state of precarious imbalance (figure 107). The direction can easily be changed by turning on the balance foot (figure 108). This is a very effective illusion!

Figure 106
Figure 107

Figure 108

The Bicycle Race

This illusion requires a great deal of effort and dynamic. Mount the bicycle in similar fashion to that described for the man's machine in the previous illustration.

The handlebars are much lower and closer together than those of a pleasure bicycle. When you are in the racing attitude, your back will be very nearly parallel to the floor and quite rounded.

In the peddling technique the feet leave the floor only minimally to move the body forward or back. The knee bends forward, draws the foot onto the ball, and immediately straightens again as the foot presses down flat onto the floor, simulating great effort.

Figure 110

Figure 109

As the one foot is flattening, the other is being drawn off the floor (figures 109 and 110).

The buttocks, while retaining fixed point in terms of height off the floor, wobble slightly from side to side as each foot is pressed to the floor. The rapidity of the rhythm and the degree of effort suggest the speed at which the bike is travelling.

A very realistic bicycle race can be suggested by two cyclists. As the feet alternate from one to the other, a slight travelling, either ahead or to the rear, is accomplished by creeping one foot a little to the front or behind the other. One cyclist can then creep ahead or fall behind the other.

The Rope: Tug-of-War

Of the three directions in which a rope may be pulled, to the side, from below and above, we will deal with the side pull first, usually, but not necessarily, a situation somewhat like a tug-of-war (figure 111).

Stand with your feet comfortably apart, facing the rope which lies on the floor in front of your toes. Let us assume it will be pulled from the left to the right. Lift the rope in the fashion of the baton, except that the back of the left hand is facing the floor. Bend both knees, body facing front, head facing over the left shoulder. Both knees are bent to the sides and pressed open. The left arm is extended out to the left side, the hand at waist level. Both hands are fixed point about shoulder width apart, the imaginary rope parallel to the floor. Without moving the feet, move the body horizontally to the right until the left leg is straight, pulling on the imaginary rope with the body, arms extended. Now, bend the elbows and pull with the muscles of the arms. At the same time pull the body back to the left side until the right leg is straight.

When the hands are at a point about the midriff, stop pulling with the arms and, with the right hand, establish a new fixed point by reaching well to the left of the body. Follow immediately with a new fixed point by means of the left hand reaching past the right. The body is now further extended to the left than at the start, and you begin again. Pull with the arms extended, moving the body to the right, until the left leg is straight and repeat the pattern. Each time you change the fixed point hand, give a pronounced impulse of effort to compensate for the fact that at that precise moment you have only one hand on the rope, and are therefore at the weakest and most vulnerable moment.

This is an effective illusion when pulling against imaginary opponents. It is also effective when performed in unison with others, but it requires extremely sensitive co-operation in order to co-ordinate the give and take of rope. The result is worth the practice.

Figure 111

The Rope: Drawing from a Well

You should have a clear picture of the well. If it is a turn-handle type, then it is a simple matter of rotating the handle a sufficient number of turns until the bucket has cleared the rim of the well, and you are free to manipulate it in whatever fashion you wish.

If the bucket is to be raised by a rope with the hands, the audience must be convinced that you are pulling the rope vertically up from below (figure 112), with the effort that is required to lift the weight of a pail filled with water (figure 113). They should see you release the excess rope to your left or right side as it becomes slack, by opening your hand, and they must be convinced that you grasp the rope each time with the appropriate dynamic to suggest the weight (figure 114).

In these functional illusions it is essential that the actor's belief in the weight and the resistance of the objects is extremely well established.

Figure 112

Figure 114

Figure 113

The Rope: Church Bells

Here again, the belief in the function and action of a bell rope is fundamental (figure 115). The technique is to reach up high over your head with, first say, the left hand, establishing a fixed point, and then the right hand establishing a fixed point vertically below the left and at a position about forehead level (figure 116). With a dynamic accent, pull down with the weight of the body, arms staying in fixed relation to each other, until the knees have bent considerably. From this point the arm muscles will pull the rope a further distance down (figure 117).

Figure 116

Figure 115

Figure 117

Return now in the reverse direction. First the arms, then the knees, straighten to elongate the body, until you are extended up onto your toes (figure 118). Continue to pull the rope in the same fashion, each pull a little lower than the last, and each return elongating you more and more until you are literally pulled into the air by the retracting rope, and your feet are off the ground.

Now reverse the order of the procedure until the bells slow down and stop ringing. It is important that the two fixed-point hands stay at the same relevant distance from each other throughout the illusion.

Figure 118

Climbing a Ladder

Imagine a universal ladder. The rungs are round, about half a metre wide and a little less than half a metre apart. The ladder is standing against a wall a metre out from the base and rises four metres high.

Starting from the neutral state (figure 119), begin by establishing three fixed points: one with each hand in baton fashion, about shoulder width apart, on the rung just above the head (figures 120 and 121); and a third, the right foot on a rung at a position slightly in front of and at the height of the left knee (figure 122). These three points move in unison and the distance they move is governed by the height of the foot from the floor. The moment the foot reaches the floor, the three points must stop (figure 123).

Pull the weight of the body up as you pull the three fixed points down. To enhance this feeling of rising, as you pull the two hands and push the left foot down, quickly go up onto the ball of the right foot, then immediately flatten it again, sending a subtle undulation throughout the length of the body.

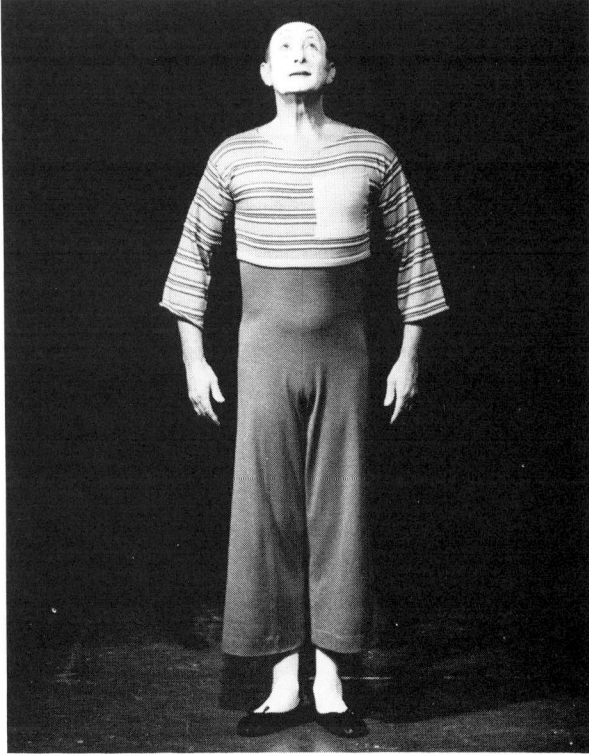

Figure 119

Figure 120

Figure 121

Figure 122

Figure 123

Now release and re-establish the left hand at a point where the next rung would be, above the other. Again this should be just above the head (figure 124).

Now take the right hand and re-establish it to the right of the left hand (figure 125). Lift the left foot up and place it, fixed point, next to the right knee and a little in front of it (figure 126). Repeat the pulling down motions as before, and rise as before, this time onto the right foot. Immediately flatten it again.

These specifics can be repeated three or four times, until you are familiar with them. Then you are free to use the vertical members of the ladder, instead, to place your hands. In this case the hands need not be horizontal to each other as they were when you were using the horizontal rungs. The foot movements are the same. You may also, at this time, prefer to use a hand-over-hand technique for variation.

Figure 125

Figure 124

Figure 126

As you arrive at the top of the ladder, sustain the last two hand fixed points, as the alternate feet do three exchanges. In other words, without repositioning your hands, pull them down to the usual position at shoulder level, then to a lower position at waist level, and lastly to a position just below the knees. At this point you release the hands and step over the final rung and straighten up. You might indicate a slight imbalance upon attaining an insecure height.

At some point within the illusion you could convey the height you have reached from the ground, and the distance still to climb, simply by looking down and up, allowing your face to reflect your feelings (figure 127).

Climbing a Wall

This is a most difficult illusion to create as it involves the attempt to bring an established level, the top of a wall, from a height over your head, down to the level of the floor upon which you stand. With practice and precise rhythms it can be very effective within the context of a sketch. Out of context it tends to appear mechanical.

Begin by establishing the illusion of the wall, just in front of you: stand looking at the top, assuming the wall is slightly over two metres high (figure 128). Jump symmetrically up, extending the arms to the sides and up, reaching for the top of the imaginary wall (figure 129). Land, flat-footed, a short distance forward: at that precise moment, slap the right-angled hands fixed point on the top of the wall, about shoulder-width apart. Your hands and feet must land simultaneously. Your arms are fully extended and the feeling is that your body is now suspended, hanging from the wall.

Figure 127

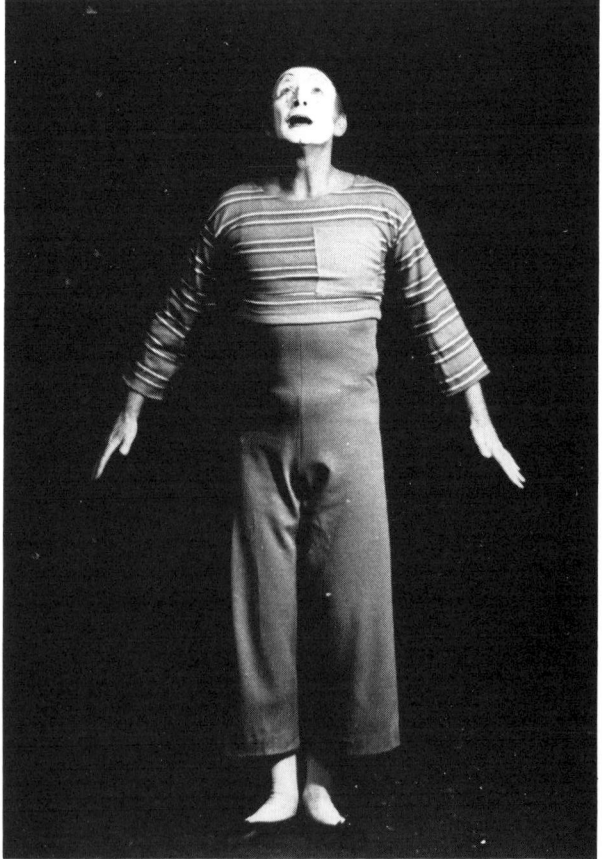

Figure 128

Continue the illusion of raising your body by pulling yourself symmetrically up with both arms. Your elbows will bend outward to both sides and then fold back in, along the sides of the rib cage, to a point where the hands are now just below the chin, and you can theoretically see over your wall (figure 130, 131 and 132). This move should be smooth, and reflect the considerable effort of pulling your body up against the resistance of gravity.

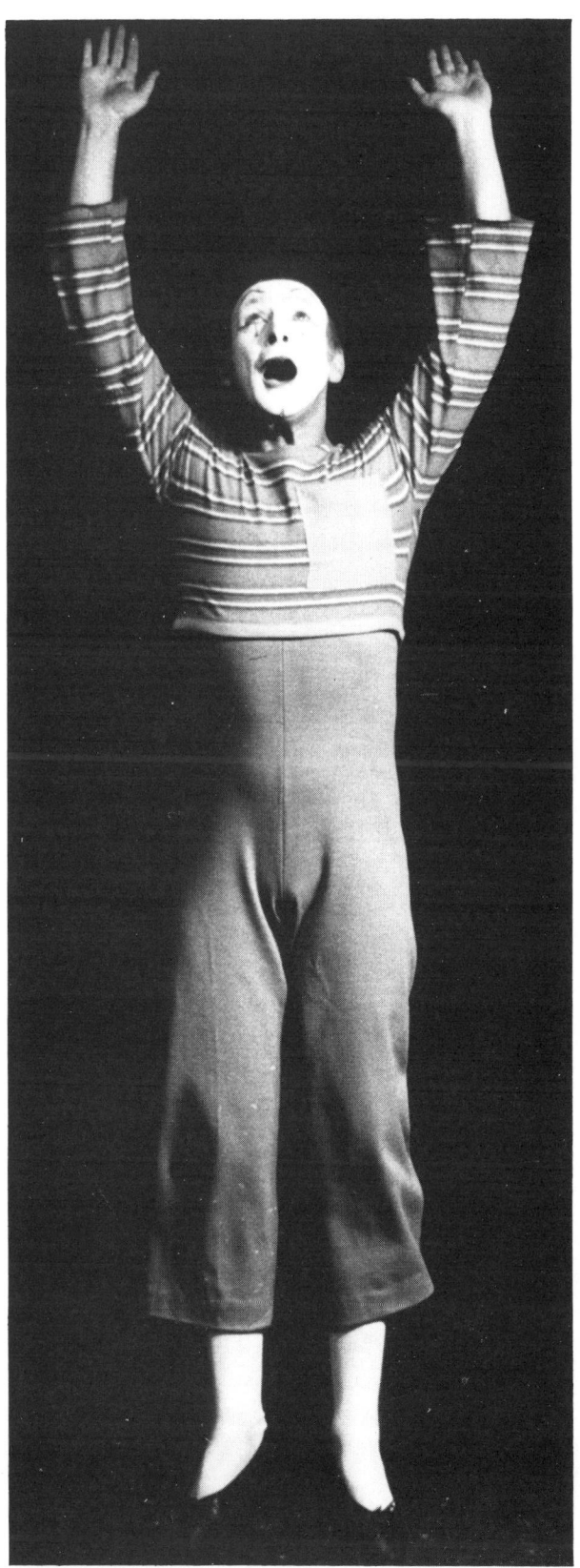

Figure 129

Figure 130

Figure 131

Figure 132

As you pull yourself up, slowly rise onto the balls of both feet and balance there. It will help you to balance if you lock the heels against each other (figure 133).

The next two moves should follow in rapid succession. First, raise the right elbow and flatten the right-angled hand and turn it inward a little. In order to do this, the elbow rises at a high outward angle. Secondly, rapidly follow this with similar movements of the left elbow and hand (figure 134).

Now, very smoothly and without leaning forward, push the two flat hands downward, allowing the thumbs actually to touch your body, until you arms are straight. Your hands should be parallel to the floor. Continue to balance on the balls of both feet (figure 135). Your hands will continue to move down as you execute the following foot movements.

Figure 133

These movements will eventually be executed at a rapid rhythm. Pivot your left foot inward and flatten it to the floor. At the same time, lift the right foot and place it flat on top of the imaginary wall, in line with the two flat hands which have now reached the knee level (figure 136). Continue to lower the three fixed points, the hands and right foot, keeping them even and horizontal until they reach the floor (figure 137). Take the right hand off the floor, and place the left foot where the hand has been, as if bringing it from a lower level. Straighten up, indicating the difficulty of regaining your balance, now that you are standing on top of the wall, and recover (figure 138 and 139).

Depending on the situation, you could now walk along the top of the wall in tight-rope fashion; jump off the wall down to the other side; or dive down as if it were holding back a body of water. These last two illusions follow.

Figure 135

Figure 134

Figure 136

Figure 137

Figure 138   Figure 139

Jumping Off a Height

This is also an illusion which, in context, can work very well, but it too depends a great deal on the actor's belief, and the rhythms with which it is effected.

Standing on top of your imaginary height, probably a wall, psyche yourself into a state that will give you the necessary courage to jump, as you look down, by relating to the imaginary space through which you must fall (figure 140 and 141).

Figure 141

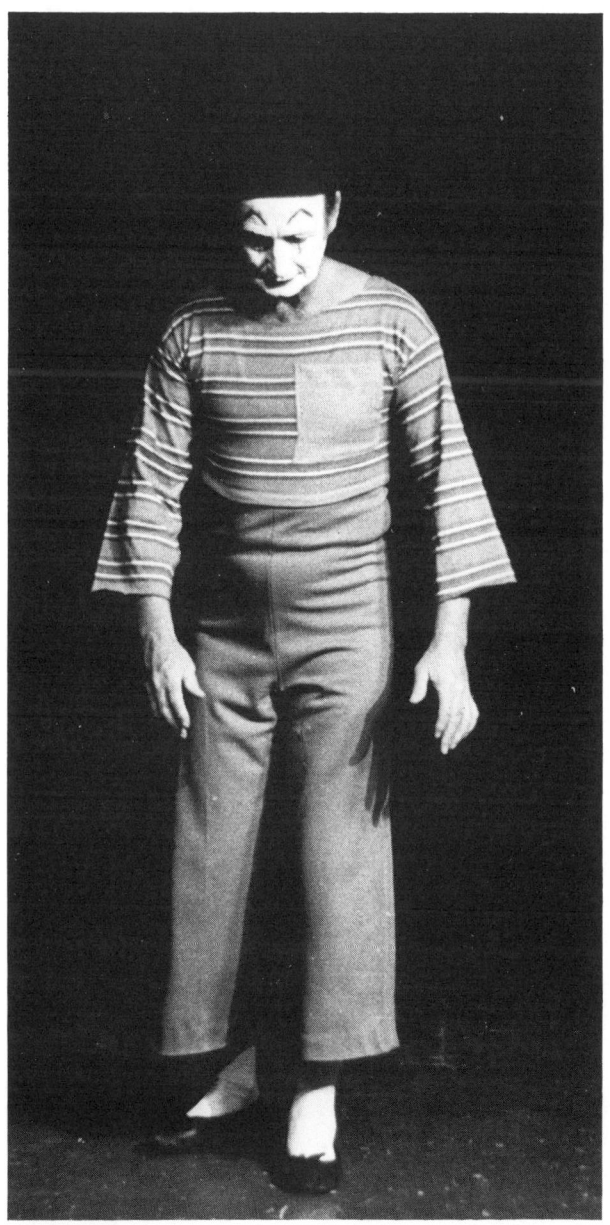

Figure 140

Make the decision to jump and, in a controlled manner, throw yourself up and out into the imaginary space (figure 142), balancing on the balls of your feet, extending both arms over your head, and elongating the body as much as possible. Hold this extended attitude in stillness for a beat or two (figure 143).

With a quickening rhythm, begin to turn and bend at the knees so that you accept the floor with the side of the leg, then the side of the knee (figure 144), and finally the side of the haunches. Only then start to lower the arms asymmetrically, and place the hands on the floor to break your fall as the body bends and also touches the floor (figure 145).

Figure 142

Figure 143

Figure 144

Figure 145

Quickly turn the head and look back up at the top of the wall from which you have just jumped. Immediately turn back and rise, accepting your new environment.

Coup de Poisson: The Dive

This illusion is a brilliant one and should only be attempted by those who have some proficiency in acrobatics, and are able to do a very controlled handstand.

Stand on the wall, or a diving board, or whatever the situation requires (figure 146).

Prepare yourself with the necessary concentration and the physical attitude.

Spring into a handstand and hold it stationary for a beat of two or three counts (figure 147).

Arch the back in an extreme fashion and slowly lower your body by bending the arms and elbows until the floor is accepted first by the chest (figure 148), then by the abdomen and finally the legs and knees (figure 149). At this point, twist onto one side and, as if underwater, swim with your arms as you rise up and your head breaks the surface (figures 150 to 153).

Along with tremendous control, the actor's belief is needed to establish the colour necessary for this illusion.

Figure 146   Figure 147

Figure 148   **Figure 149**

Figure 150   **Figure 151**

Figure 152

Figure 153

Swimming in Place

This is a simple illusion and, if done well, can be very effective, particularly if it develops out of an illusion such as the dive.

Stand balanced on one leg as in the star exercise. Elongate the body parallel to the floor.

For the breast stroke, simulate the swimming motion with your arms going forward and out to the sides and back (figure 154). At the same time, with one free leg, do the frog kick by bending your knee forward and to the side, then kicking back. Synchronize the legs with the forward motion of your arms (figure 155).

For the Australian crawl and overhand stroke, again simply simulate the real movements and add a one-leg kick or a flutter kick with the free foot.

Figure 154

Figure 155

PART IV
Solos, Ensembles, Mimodrama

Solos, Ensembles, Mimodrama

At certain stages of your development, you will want to test your competence in the skills by doing sketches and plays. The following are a number of pieces designed for this purpose. They are presented in two forms: first, as a précis on the theme or situation; and, second, in the developed and detailed form that a finished piece must take.

First, examine the précis only and improvise around the characters and the situation. Have an instructor or student director guide the rehearsals. Initial attempts may be chaotic, but as the director chooses certain moments and discards others, a shape will eventually evolve.

Secondly, take the developed piece as presented, and, with your director, rehearse, phrase by phrase, each moment as it progresses. Realize how meticulously every detail must be thought out and rehearsed. In this way you will learn to work out and plan the themes created by your own imagination.

The principles to be stressed are: the ability to remain still, a passive but dynamic inner state; the giving and taking of focus; concentration and knowing your objective on stage; and relating with an actor's belief to the actions and reactions and the circumstances as they unfold within the piece. Your skills and techniques will become more precise and economical as you strengthen your muscle tone and develop flexibility.

A Solo

Don't Pick the Flowers

Précis

One set piece, a sign: "Don't Pick the Flowers"

A man of extreme emotions, ranging from joy to tragedy, who loves everything beautiful, picks some flowers before he notices a sign reading, "Don't Pick the Flowers."

Guiltily he tries to return the flowers to their original spot, but on reflection decides to defy authority and savours the fragrance of the last flower in his hands. He plays "she loves me, she loves me not" and the petals decide in his favour. Ecstatically, he fantasizes about a beautiful girl, dancing with her until he becomes overly amorous. She slaps his face and disappears from his imagination.

Dejected, he picks another flower and plays the game again. This time he loses. Utterly downcast, he decides to end his life. First he tries to stab himself with a dagger but he discards it because it is too frightening. Then he finds a rope and attempts to hang himself but he throws it away when he can find no place to tie it. As he looks around for still other methods, he trips on the rope and falls, impaling himself on the dagger. He realizes that this is the ultimate retribution and picks another flower, offering it symbolically to the authoritarian sign, and dies.

Mimedrama

One set piece, a sign: "Don't Pick the Flowers" DSR

The mime enters from SR (Stage Right), energetically crosses to SL (Stage Left) and notices an imaginary plot of, flowers across the apron. This slows him and brings him DSL (Down Stage Left) as he goes into raptures over the beauty of the flowers. He picks one DSL and revels in its aroma. Quickly, he picks one DSC (Down Stage Centre) and adds it to the one in his left hand.

He continues to DSR (Down Stage Right) and picks a third, then freezes in his bent-over position as he becomes aware of the sign. He turns his head to read it, then, still in the bent-over position, does a "take" to the audience. Quickly he tries to replant the flowers DSR and DSC.

He is about to do the same DSL, but stops with his hand raised. As he slowly straightens up, the guilt drains out of him, and, gradually, he assumes a feeling of rebellion. He is determined to defy the sign.

Delighting in the fragrance of the flower, he catches his breath as an idea occurs to him. He plucks a petal from the flower, playing "she loves me." Pleased, he flicks it into space, and the flower petal slowly zig-zags to the ground. He follows it with his head and eyes. He plucks a second petal — "she loves me not" — and is dejected. He quickly plucks another "yes" and then another "no" and, with great anticipation, a final "yes" petal.

He flicks the last petal into the air as he does an impulsive turn in place and hugs himself at the thought of a beautiful girl in love with him. Suddenly he sees her materializing above his head and floating down to stand in front of him. To him she is real.

Gallantly he kisses her hand and suggests, with a gesture, that they dance. She is SR of him. He takes first her imaginary left hand and puts it behind his neck, then her right hand and extends it as the guiding dance arm. He places his right hand behind her waist. He does a three-step waltz to SR, returns centre, and turns a few times in place.

As he manoeuvres her upstage of himself, he raises both arms and impulsively embraces her. The right hand goes up behind her imaginary left ear and strokes the back of her head. The left hand goes under her right arm and strokes her body from the shoulder down to below the hip.

Enough is enough! The right hand determinedly comes around and takes the left hand off the hip and places it back on the shoulder. The right hand then returns to stroking the back of the head. The left hand uncontrollably caresses down to below the hip. Now the right hand slaps the cheek sharply and he turns DS to see his fantasy-love disappear. He makes a futile attempt to stop her from vanishing into thin air. The above is in fact physically done by the mime himself to himself.

He is dejected. Sadly he picks the flower from DSC and, almost as if he knows what the result will be, plucks a petal ''yes,'' a petal ''no,'' a petal ''yes,'' and a final petal ''no.'' Discarding both flower and stem, he looks slowly from one hand to the other. We can see from his determination that he is considering taking his own life.

He nods imperceptibly, slowly closing his hands around his throat. Taking a deep breath that puffs his cheeks, he closes his eyes and squeezes. Two beats of rhythm go by.

He opens his eyes and looks down at his nose. He tries to pinch his nostrils with one hand and choke himself with the other. He exchanges hands, but it still does not work.

Shrugging, he gives up, and searches for another solution.

He remembers a dagger in an imaginary scabbard at his left side. With a flourish, he draws it with his right hand and holds it, point up, in front of himself. He tests its sharpness with the forefinger of his left hand and quickly sucks the little pebble of blood which it draws.

He inverts the dagger as he takes it in his left hand and, turning sideways to SL, he prods his extended abdomen with his right forefinger

to find the most likely place for the dagger to enter.

Satisfied that he has found a good spot, he takes the dagger in both hands and draws it towards him until the point touches his stomach. The extended abdomen goes from its convex state to a contracted concave state, the point of the knife moving with it at all times. He rises on his toes in an effort to stay ahead of the point, and at that moment gives up. The knife is far too frightening. Dejected, he throws the knife a little to his right.

Looking to the left, he becomes excited when he sees a rope coiled a few paces away. Quickly he takes one end and draws it to him. In a moment of elation, he does a few skips with the rope — and then remembers his grim objective.

He shapes the rope into a noose and places it over his head and around his neck, extending its length vertically with his left hand. He draws the knot down close to his neck with his right hand. This accomplished, he drops his right arm to his side, keeping it very loose. The left arm remains above his head, holding the other end of the rope. Very methodically he stretches bit by bit up onto his toes, extending himself as much as is humanly possible, and balancing for a brief moment.

Then quickly, he bends his knees a little as if he had been dropped through a trap door, closes his eyes and hangs loosely, suspending himself from his own left hand, his right arm swinging loosely. He holds this position for a count of three or four, turns his head to look upward at his hand, then out to the audience, and with a shrug of defeat, proceeds to open the noose and take it from around his neck.

Already disinterested in the rope, he looks away to his left for something else to use, carelessly dropping the rope to his right side in a tangled mess. He continues to turn upstage, still looking.

He extends both arms up and out in the classic ''nothing'' cliché. He turns back and around and, in taking a step toward SR, tangles his feet in the discarded rope and trips suddenly. He falls onto the previously discarded dagger which pierces his abdomen. He stiffens his body and supports himself on his right forearm, as he draws his left hand across his abdominal wound. Looking at his hand, he flicks the blood off.

In bewilderment he looks at the sign which is now quite near his head. He looks at the SR flower he had earlier replanted, picks it with his left hand and slowly, not really knowing why, offers it to the sign, asking forgiveness. He slumps suddenly in death.

Blackout.

A Solo

The Red Balloon

Précis

Based on the film by Albert Lamorrise, *Le Balon Rouge*.

A little boy finds a balloon. He plays with it and eventually it becomes his friend, taking on a personality of its own. A gang of boys attacks him, throwing stones at him. A stone bursts his balloon. He is heartbroken. The boys start to threaten him again and all the balloons in the world come floating through the sky to his aid. He gathers some of the balloons into his hand, holding the strings. The balloons lift him up into the sky and carry him off to safety.

Mimedrama

The boy is discovered DSR walking in place, facing L, enjoying a beautiful spring day outdoors. Suddenly his glance is riveted on something red on the ground DSL. He continues to walk in place, gradually slowing his pace as his head and eyes bring the location of the object to his feet.

He is pleased as he sees that it is a balloon not yet blown up, and he looks L and R to see if there is someone near to whom it might belong. There is no one there; he bends and picks it up.

Taking it in both hands, he stretches it, not without a degree of difficulty, further — out and in, out and in a few times to increase its elasticity. With great anticipation, he holds it with the index finger and thumb of both hands, puts it to his lips and blows a breath into it. The other fingers show the increase in the round shape of the balloon as his first breath expands it a little.

He takes it away from his lips and admires the progress so far. He takes a huge breath and brings the balloon back to his lips. He blows but, in his eagerness, the balloon escapes and zigzags around. He follows it with his head and eyes until it lands a little to his right.

He retrieves the balloon and quickly cleans the little bit of dirt from it with his sleeve. He then takes the balloon and slowly stretches it vertically until it extends an arm's length over his head with one hand to below his waist with the other hand. It slips out of his lower hand and snaps up to the other, jiggling it a bit.

Now he takes the balloon in both hands again and tests its elasticity. This time it stretches easily to almost a metre horizontally.

Very pleased with himself, he puts it to his lips with his right hand and blows several times. The left hand shapes its increase in size each time he blows into it until it is almost a metre in diameter.

He takes it away from his mouth and, bringing the other hand in, ties it off. With great pride he looks at his beautiful balloon.

He leans out to the right and gently taps the balloon into the air. It travels slowly in a gentle arc over his head to SL. He runs to it and taps it back. It travels gently to SR. He runs to it and gives it a soccer "header" and back it goes slowly to the left.

Watching the balloon continuously, he follows it across and gives it a beautiful high punt kick which sends it back over his head to SR. Now he runs under it and, turning his back, watches it descend over his shoulder, giving it a back kick at the right moment.

It goes straight up and stays in the air defiantly. He stands underneath, looking up at it, for several beats. He looks straight out, perplexed, looks back up, raises his hand, and gently beckons it down with his index finger. He holds this attitude for two beats.

When the balloon does not respond he makes a sudden command gesture, "come down," pointing to the ground with the same hand, and holding the gesture for two beats.

He relaxes and looks out. Then he gets an idea: trying to look up and see the balloon, he feigns indifference. Shrugging his shoulders, he starts to walk in place, side view, toward SL. He walks for several steps and glancing quickly back he smiles; his ruse is working, the balloon is following him.

He breaks into a run in place, quickens his tempo for several beats, then quickly breaks into a realistic run USC a few paces and hides behind an imaginary wall.

His hands are both fixed point on the wall. He travels a few paces to the right and back to centre. He peeks over the top of the wall and sees that the balloon has followed him. He quickly ducks down again.

He goes slowly to the right and establishes the end of the wall, peeking around it. Quietly he tiptoes around the wall and sneaks up on the balloon, grasping it in both hands by its considerable diameter.

He brings it to his body and, releasing his right hand, takes a string from his side pocket and shakes it out. He ties it to the balloon. Holding one end of the string, proudly and jauntily he walks in place towards SL.

Pointing to his balloon he looks out with pride to some boys who are over the stage apron DSR. Then he realizes that they are threatening him.

He pulls the balloon down by its string and puts his arms around it protectively as he backs upstage until he feels the wall. Unable to go any further, he crouches on his right knee trying to protect the balloon and himself at the same time.

He flinches a few times as the boys throw stones that land perilously close. One hits his forehead and his right arm goes up to protect it. A second stone bursts the balloon. His hand goes to the widest part of the circular shape and the two hands come together as the balloon slowly deflates.

He looks at the boys with a slight turn of the head: "Why have you done this thing?" They throw more rocks and he cowers behind his right forearm.

Over his arm he sees hundreds of balloons coming to his rescue. After a quick rhythm of looking here, there, and everywhere in the sky, he finally concentrates on one balloon floating down to him.

He stretches up and, with his right hand, draws it down to his left hand. Again he brings a second balloon down to his left hand, gathering the strings together. He reaches a final time and captures the third balloon. With both hands, he gathers the strings securely in a bunch. Slowly his hands start to rise and, as they pass his face, he smiles in wonder and amazement. His arms reach their fullest extension and his body stretches through the torso and shoulders. Finally his legs straighten as he slowly extends to his fullest height. On tiptoe, he slowly turns and floats away.

Briefly he releases his right hand for a short little wave to the boys. (*The lights fade to black and he might move offstage behind a curtain. This final illusion of being carried away is greatly enhanced if a spotlight can isolate the boy for the final few moments.*)

A Solo

The Chair

Précis

Create a physical metaphor to illustrate a situation in which the object of desire (symbolically represented by an arm chair) can control and eventually conquer the desirer.

Mimedrama

Property: **One light-weight, simple, open arm chair**

The arm chair is centre stage, well lit, alone.

The mime is propelled from SR on stage and falls to the floor DSL of the chair. He immediately recovers and dashes back SR to an imaginary obstruction that has closed off his escape. Using the wall technique he explores for some opening or flaw US and across to SL and ends DSL, exploring a little of the fourth wall before giving up. He has been unaware of the chair and completely ignores it. Deep in contemplation he casually glances at the chair and away again, then quickly snaps his head back to look for a few long moments at THIS chair.

Apparently satisfied that it is of little consequence he crosses back to SR and with less desperation examines the wall again. With his attention still on the wall he backs away close to the chair. He puts his hand out to lean on the chair for support. The moment his hand touches the chair it is flung uncontrollably away as if thrown off by the chair.

Startled, he backs off a pace USR. He looks to his hand that his been repelled and back to the chair, in disbelief. Tentatively, he reaches out and comes back to the chair. This time the moment the chair is touched, the hand is thrown away with even more force. *(Technically, the hand moves the chair away a foot or so. Care must be taken not to overturn the chair.)* The mime recovers and stands alert ready to defend himself from further attack.

There is stillness for a moment, during which we can see that he has formulated a plan. Slowly, he relaxes and feigns indifference. Casually, he crosses US of the chair to the USL area. He then quickly turns and with both arms grabs the left arm of the chair, which rocks back and forth more aggressively until the mime is thrown to the floor.

Highly angered he regains his feet and takes the chair from behind in a full-Nelson wrestling hold. There is a great use of space as the chair seemingly struggles to be free of the mime until a moment, punctuated by several resistances from the chair, when the chair finally remains still, CS.

Cautiously, the mime releases one part of his hold on the chair and takes a new one as he slowly works his way to the front of the chair. At the same time he works his body into a seated position in the chair. Once or twice there can be a weak resistance from the chair, subdued immediately by the mime.

Finally seated properly, he begins to caress the arms of the chair, becoming sensuously enamoured of the chair. He works progressively and slowly each of his arms under, through and over each arm of the chair, and each of his legs back, through and around each leg of the chair. He is pleasantly, sensuously and smilingly immersed by the chair. Throughout this last phase there has been a subtle undulating of the mime's body. Finally satiated, the mime becomes still.

He makes a move to get up. He can't. He tries again. He can't. He makes a third tremendous effort to extricate himself. He can't. Looking straight out, we see the slow comprehension coming over the face of the mime. Slowly, the face breaks into a horrendous silent scream as he arches his back and gives a final effort to free himself. (*The lights go to black.*)

A Solo

The Impressionist

Précis

On a hot day, an artist of the impressionists school draws a painting of a natural setting. The heat is so oppressive and the painting so real that he solves his dilemma by taking a swim in the ocean he has painted.

Mimedrama

The artist enters USR carrying under his left arm a folded tripod easel and in his right hand the handle of his paint case containing his tubes of paint, a palette and brushes. He comes DS a little and looks out over the audience in an outdoor setting. He sets the paint case on the ground and looks skyward to the sun. He wipes the perspiration from his forehead with the sleeve of his forearm and shows his discomfort with the heat of the day. He takes the easel from under his arm and opens it up, setting it DSC. He then goes to the exact spot where he left the paints case and shakes out a folding legs contraption that enables the case to be on its own support, and places it steady on the ground to his right. He reacts to the sun and its heat again.

He opens the lid of the case, much like a briefcase top and takes out his palette. He places his left thumb through the palette opening and turns the board to rest along his forearm. He takes a tube of paint with his right hand from the case and for a moment is in a quandry as to how to meet the conflict of the left engaged hand and the need to unscrew the cap off the tube of paint. With a smug little self-satisfied smile he registers an idea and putting the cap in his mouth he unscrews the tube clockwise, freeing the tube in his right hand and leaving the cap in his teeth. He spits the cap away with a flick of his head. He squeezes the tube of blue paint onto his palette in a big blob and shakes the last of it out of the tube and tosses it away. He takes another and does the same but does not spit the cap away. This time he squeezes just a few drops of black onto another area, then puts the tube back into the cap in his mouth and screws the tube counterclockwise back into it, and replacing it in the paints case. He repeats this quickly with another tube of orange paint and returns that tube to the case. He reacts to the heat of the sun again.

He takes a brush from the case and gathers a brushload of blue and describes a perfect rectangle on a flat plane with the easel. He takes great care to keep the top line absolutely horizontal to the horizon and describes a line a good four feet in length. A little more paint and he draws the right-hand vertical line at right angles to the top line, about three feet deep. Taking more paint he continues in this fashion to complete the outline of the rectangle. Once again, he relates to the heat of the sun.

He looks out around the side of his ethereal canvas looking for a subject to paint. He sees the distant ocean and shows his pleasure. He suggests the liquidity in motions through his right arm, quickly takes on some blue paint in his brush and about mid-distance down his canvas he draws an obvious wavy line from left to right and repeats it several times a few inches apart until he fills the bottom half of the canvas filling his brush from time to time. He stands back and admires his progress so far. He relates again to the heat.

He looks far out for further subject matter, smiles when he sees a flock of birds and with his elbows simulates a few beats of the gulls wings. He takes a meticulous dab of black onto his brush and in the upper right expanse of his canvas he draws several little lines to suggest he wings of birds in the distance. He relates to the sun again and as he wipes his brow he gets an idea and does a quick

The Canadian Mime Theatre in a sketch by the Author, *The Pub*, see Page 139

double take to the sun. He smiles and quickly takes some orange on his brush. In the centre of his canvas he draws a fairly large perfect circle and then draws a series of short and longer lines radiating out from the circumference of the sun. Again, he stands back to admire his painting. Once again, he reacts to the heat of the real sun.

Then he gets an idea. With a feeling of going to do something forbidden he looks offstage, left and right. He quickly puts his brush and palette back in the case. He begins to undress, taking off an upper garment and his trousers each time, folding them precisely and resting them on his case. He realizes how vulnerable he is, naked, and attempts to hide himself by crossing his hands in front of himself. He takes the outer edges of his canvas and lifts it off the easel. He turns it flat to the floor and lowers it to about knee height from the floor. He steps over the side into the painting as if it is water. He feels and flicks the cold water over his face and shoulders reacting to the refreshing feeling. He stands and turns to face SL. He reaches down and taking the edges of the canvas and lifts it until it is shoulder high. He holds his nose and ducks down in the water. Then he swims up to the surface and swims in place facing off SL until the lights fade to black.

A Duet

Painless Dentistry
Précis

A dentist with a slightly sadistic streak receives an extremely timid patient with a very low pain threshold. The dentist tries every modern pain relief at his disposal to calm the patient, but each time he attempts to work on him the patient is panic-stricken.

Finally, the dentist remembers an old tank of nitrous oxide hidden away in a cupboard. He manages to put the patient to sleep but, as he attempts to turn the tank off, the valve handle breaks and gas floods the room, sending the dentist into rapturous laughter and delight at the helplessness of his patient. Carried away, he extracts, not just the patient's aching tooth, but all of them.

He awakens the patient to show him his face in the mirror, amid fits of hysterical laughter. The patient slaps the dentist on the back, dislodging the dentist's false teeth, which he retrieves.

The patient has fun trying out the doctor's teeth and darts out of the office, leaving the doctor to realize that, now, he is toothless.

Mimedrama

Players	Slightly sadistic dentist. Wears a doctor's smock.
	Very timid patient with low pain threshold. Wears a kerchief tied over his head and painfully swollen jaw.
Properties	For the major portion of the sketch there will be a seat positioned just left of centre stage. It can be a chair with a back upon which the patient can ideally tilt back; or it can be a bare stool upon which the patient will lean back balancing securely with his hands or feet, with the base or legs of the stool as support.

Standing by his chair straightening his tools on an imaginary shelf DSL, the dentist swivels the retractable table from in front of the chair, moves it a little closer to the shelf, and methodically lays out certain tools on it in preparation for his first patient of the day.

He takes an imaginary pair of pliers and works them open and closed several times before replacing them on the table. Then he takes what is obviously a probe and twists it through the air as if he were reaming out the dry-socket of some helpless patient. From the expression on his face it is evident that he delights in inflicting pain.

He places the probe on the tray, turns straight DS, and with both hands lifts and slightly adjusts a mirror which is leaning against the shelf. A certain narcissism shows as he sleeks back his hair while admiring his appearance in the mirror. He smiles at his reflection, especially his teeth.

A look of consternation crosses his face as he quickly peers more closely into the mirror. With his fingernail he tries to scrape a blemish off one of his front teeth, wiping the spot with his tongue. Putting his hand to his mouth he pretends to take out his denture, holding his lips taut to hide his real teeth. He takes an instrument from his tray and vigorously scrapes the plate, replaces his denture and with a toothy smile again admires his reflection in the mirror.

A sharp turn of his head to the USR corner indicates that he has heard someone at the door. In a business-like manner he straightens his sleeves, brushes back his hair, and flicks his smock while going up to the imaginary USR door. He opens it wide with a ''come in'' gesture, steps back a pace and freezes.

Patient
Pathetically and slowly enters through the imaginary door, turns to face DS, and points to his aching, bandaged jaw.

From the Canadian Mime Theatre production of *Painless Dentistry*. The unsuspecting patient is played by Harro Maskow, the sadistic dentist by Adrian Pecknold.

Dentist
Mesmerized at this sight, is drawn to point at the swelling, almost touching it.

Patient
Startled at this proximity puts his hand to his jaw and moves as if to leave.

Dentist
Grabs him quickly by the elbow and draws him into the office, indicating the chair. The dentist then closes the door quickly and returns to the patient in time to coax him physically into the chair. He puts the usual apron on with a flourish and ties it behind the neck.

He pats the patient reassuringly on the shoulder and, putting his right hand near the patient's right shoulder, the dentist pumps an imaginary handle back and forth (more like a barber's chair than a dentist's, but the licence is defensible and it is very funny). At the same time the patient gradually tilts the chair back, stopping when the dentist stops pumping.

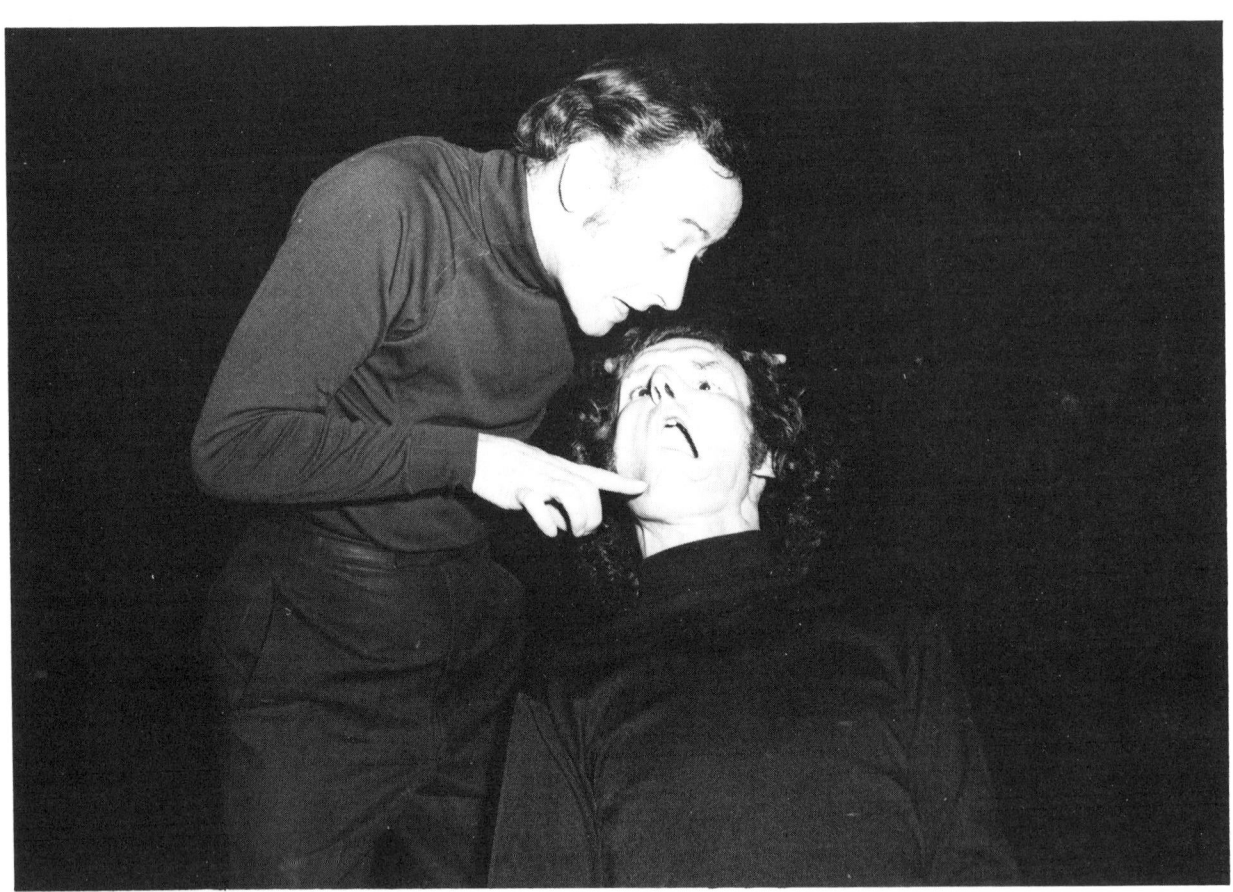

The dentist then slips the kerchief off the patient's head and puts it in his own pocket without drawing attention to it. He leans down and forward and indicates "tut-tut" by shaking his head in a slow negative manner, as if to say: "This is the worst case of toothache I have ever encountered."

Patient
Who has been staring at the dentist's face, looks slowly out front with a glazed, frightened look, swallowing in fear.

Dentist
Swings the retractable tray over the front of the patient. He takes the little long-handled mirror, blows on it, and polishes it vigorously on the sleeve of his smock. Checking his work, he can't resist a narcissistic look at his own reflection. He sleeks his hair down before turning to the patient and indicating that he open his mouth.

Patient
Looking at the dentist out of the corner of his eye, slowly obliges, and the dentist turns the mirror this way and that as he searches for the offending tooth.

Dentist
Takes the mirror away and puts it on the tray. He leans forward and down again, nodding his head, and is about to point at and touch the tender jaw.

Patient
Holding his jaw protectively, draws back and away from the dentist to remind him that he has had no pain killer as yet.

Dentist
Nodding affirmatively, he takes a needle from the tray with his right hand and a bottle of Novocaine in his left. About to insert the needle into the top of the bottle he pauses, realizing that it might be prudent for the patient not to see this. Turning his back, the dentist inserts the needle and draws a quantity of fluid from the bottle by holding it high and allowing the thumb plunger to be pulled back out. To ensure that there is no air in the needle, he gives a couple of little squirts in the prescribed manner as he replaces the bottle on the tray. He then attempts to open the patient's mouth.

Patient
Once again turns his head quickly away in absolute panic.

Dentist
Patiently and as reassuringly as possible, gently reaches out and turns the patient's head back toward him. Then, putting his thumb on the cleft of the chin, he forces the jaw down and the mouth open. Just as he stabs the patient with the needle . . .

Patient
Snaps his head away with the result that . . .

Dentist
Sticks his own thumb with the needle. In excruciating pain the dentist backs away to CS and pulls the needle out of his thumb. Slowly recovering his composure, and shaking his thumb, he turns to look at the patient as if he would like to kill him.

Patient
Gulps in fear and remains in his drawn back attitude.

Dentist
In the meantime, his hand has frozen in a grotesquely deformed manner which he notices for the first time as he again tries to open the patient's mouth with his thumb. This occasions a double-take and he is forced to use his left elbow to pry open the patient's mouth. Finally he is able to inject the drug — not gently, but with a vicious jab.

Patient
Is tense and trembles during the injection. He relaxes when the dentist withdraws the needle.

Dentist
Still looking angrily at the patient, returns the needle to the tray and then one by one, forces some sense of feeling back to the thumb and fingers of his left hand, straightening them and pounding them with his right fist.

Finally satisfied, he extends both palms toward the patient in a "hands off" attitude. He checks his watch and is about to test the effectiveness of the drug when once again . . .

Patient
Draws back in great fear.

Dentist

In exasperation, goes quickly USL to a cupboard behind the patient on the SL wall, opens it, and removes a bottle, leaving the bottle cap on the imaginary sideboard. He then returns to the right side of the patient, and shaking a pill out into his left hand, offers it to the patient, and indicates the water fountain that rises from the retractable tray.

Patient

Takes the pill with his right hand and the paper cup of water in his left and swallows the pill. They both wait a couple of seconds to observe the effect. The patient holds out his empty right hand to indicate ''one more please.''

Dentist

With an upward roll of the eyes, consents. He flicks one pill from the bottle into his left hand and then turns the palm down with a flick.

Patient

Catches the imaginary pill with his right hand and takes it with another gulp of water. They now wait for a further testing period.

Dentist

Makes the slightest move toward the patient who anticipates it and draws back. With disgust and impatience, the dentist upturns the bottle of pills and shakes them all into his open right hand, then forces them into the patient's mouth.

Patient

Has a mouthful of pills and quickly takes more water to wash them down.

Dentist

During this episode, goes back to the cupboard, replaces the cap on the bottle, puts it back into the cupboard and closes the doors. He stands there for a moment, watching the patient compose himself. Then he inches his left hand to the left side of the patient's face and taps the cheek to test it.

Patient

Jumps a mile (with control) and puts his hand to his cheek in great pain.

Dentist

Contrite, tries to compose the patient by rapidly patting the top of his head. This he gradually slows to a tap, tap, as a fiendish idea occurs to him and he begins to gloat. Very cautiously, he opens a drawer below the cupboard and withdraws a baton-like weapon. Taking careful aim, he strikes the top of the patient's head.

Patient

Listens for the tap of the dentist's foot, which he has timed with the blow. On this cue the patient responds physically with quite an apparent nod of the head but emotionally shows no discomfort from the blow except a rather vacant stare out front.

Dentist

Waits a beat or so to confirm that the patient feels no pain. Quickly and with satisfaction, he returns the baton to the drawer and moves down to the right side of the patient, rubbing his hands in glee. He takes the pliers from the table, watches how well they work as he opens and closes them, as if to extract the tooth.

Patient

Seeing this weapon, once again becomes panic-stricken and pulls away from the dentist.

Dentist

Throws his hands in the air in desperation. He pauses and looks quickly to SR, a smile spreading slowly over his face. He puts the pliers back on the table, cautions the patient to wait and, taking some keys from his pocket, goes SR to an imaginary cupboard. Unlocking the door and opening it, he brushes aside the accumulated cobwebs, bends to lift, with difficulty, an old tank of laughing gas, long forgotten. He manoeuvres it to SC, then returns to close the cupboard door.

Re-approaching the tank, he rubs his hands in anticipation and lifts a coil and mask off the tank, shaking out the coil to untangle it. He returns to the patient, places the mask over his face, and ties it off behind his neck.

The dentist returns to the tank and with a gesture cautioning the patient to wait a minute, tries to turn the valve at the top of the tank. It will not budge, he tries again. It still will not turn.

He goes to the drawer, gets a blunt hammer, and returns to the tank. He gives it a well-aimed blow and places the hammer on an imaginary US table.

He then turns the valve quickly counter-clockwise for several turns. *(A hissing sound effect and laughing-mood music can be extremely effective at this moment.)* Returning to the patient, he checks his watch, then glances at the gauge on the tank. He encourages the patient to breathe deeply.

Patient

Who has been watching all this in wide-eyed terror, now begins to smile. He breathes deeply, the smile broadens. His shoulders begin to shake and he starts laughing, in silent hysteria, until he passes out. His eyes close; his head drops to the side, limp.

Dentist

Quickly double checks his watch and the tank gauge. He removes the patient's mask and begins to wind the coil around the thumb and elbow of his left arm in a series of loops. This action draws him toward the tank. When he has almost finished winding the coil, his glance falls on the mask in his left hand.

He stops for a beat as he tries to remember the feeling and effect of the gas from the old days. Unable to resist the temptation, he places the mask in his left hand over his face and inhales deeply.

Quickly he pulls his face back with a "whew" gesture and a broad laugh. He hangs the mask and coil on its hook on the tank, then rapidly turns the valve clockwise to shut it off and takes a step toward the patient.

He stops abruptly and looks back at the valve, which obviously has not shut off. With a great effort he tries to tighten it, but is unsuccessful. He laughs. He tries again, laughs.

Disoriented by the gas, he can no longer remember how to close the valve. He muses over the problem, using his index finger to indicate the direction of clockwise and counter-clockwise. Still laughing, he can't make a decision.

He quickly gets the hammer from the US table behind him, aims and strikes the valve.

He tosses the hammer back on the table and with great effort tries to tighten the valve with both hands. It snaps off in his hand. He looks at it, laughs uproariously, and tosses it on the US table.

He returns to the patient and straightens his head so it is upright. Placing two fingers of his left hand on the painful jaw, he strikes them with great force with two fingers of his right hand. The patient shows no reaction.

"Success at last!" he thinks as he gets the pliers again, opens the patient's mouth wide, and attempts to extract the tooth. The tooth proves more difficult to remove than he anticipated. He places his foot on the patient's legs to hold him down and, using both hands, extracts the tooth. He holds it up in the pliers and, with great delight, takes the tooth and carefully but rather drunkenly places it on the retractable table.

He turns to the patient with a hand gesture of "all finished." For the first time he realizes the utter helplessness of the patient. He looks at him for a couple of long beats, then begins to shake with laughter at the thought which has crossed his mind.

He comes close to the patient and peers into his mouth, then reels back in laughter. He cups the patient's mouth with his left hand and rhythmically begins to extract all his teeth, tossing them over his shoulder in all directions. *(Seven or eight teeth will suffice.)*

He replaces the pliers on the table and slaps the patient across the face a few times to wake him up.

Patient

Wakes up. Keeping his upper and lower lips drawn to hide his own teeth, he works his mouth as he rises and begins to shake the dentist's hand in thanks. They look at each other for a moment.

Dentist

Laughs and points at the patient's mouth, motioning him to wait a minute, then runs US and back down to where he had earlier established the mirror. He lifts the mirror in both hands, brings it down to the left of the patient, and offers it to him.

Patient
Takes the mirror in both hands and looks blankly at his toothless mouth.

Dentist
Points and laughs uproariously at the poor man and starts to take the mirror from him.

Patient
Laughing, allows the dentist to take it. As the dentist turns away to put the mirror back, the patient gives him a huge, good humoured slap on the back.

Dentist
His head has been slightly turned toward the patient, and the slap dislodges both his denture plates. He immediately covers his own teeth with drawn lips. Since his hands are occupied with the mirror, he points with his foot to his plates on the floor, obviously asking the patient to pick them up.

Patient
Seeing the humour in the situation, makes them bite rapidly like joke-store dentures. He places them in his own mouth, bites and smiles broadly.

Dentist
Nods "Yes, yes, that is very funny, now give back my teeth," but the patient waves him away. His hands are still occupied with the mirror. In order to free them, he is forced to return the mirror to the DS bench where he first established it.

The patient seeing that the dentist is far away, gives a few chomps on his new false teeth and runs out the door.

The dentist sees the reflection of the patient leaving in the mirror and dashes after him but gives up at the door and returns to the chair, weeping and moving his toothless mouth in abject misery to a black out.

Adrian Pecknold as the sadistic dentist and Harro Maskow as the unwitting patient in *Painless Dentistry*.

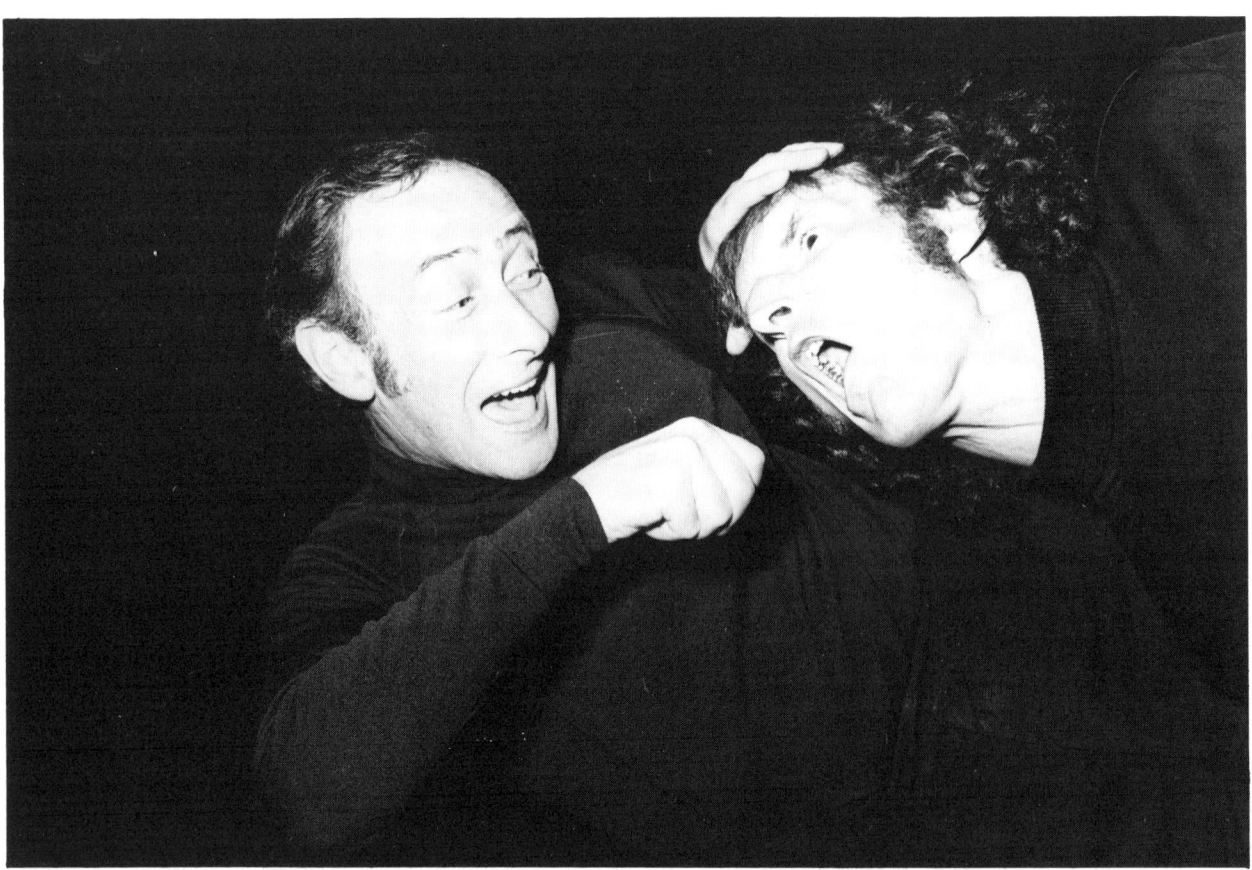

A Duet

Neighbours

Setting

Two boxes simulate chairs, one SLC, the other SRC. An imaginary wall runs from USC to DSC, with doors into the apartments immediately left and right of the imaginary wall. The hallway runs across the complete US, from right to left. There are imaginary windows left and right DS fronting the apron. The imaginary kitchen and cupboard areas are to the off side of each respective chair.

Mimedrama

Players	Mr. Left
	Mr. Right

Properties	two boxes

Mr. Left
Enters from USR and goes to the left door. He is carrying a newspaper under his arm. He takes his keys from his pocket, opens the door and enters his apartment. He turns on the light switch to his immediate right on the imaginary wall. His nose does a little sniff at the staleness of the room.

He tosses the imaginary paper onto the chair and proceeds DS to the window. He unfastens the catch and opens the window wide up. He pokes his head out, looks down and to the left and right and inhales a deep breath. He has been careful of a potted plant on the window sill. He lifts it, smells its fragrance, notices a blemished leaf, picks if off and flicks it out the window. He replaces the plant on the sill and goes to the side cupboard.

He opens a cupboard and takes a glass and a bottle of scotch and pours himself a drink. He gives it a splash of water from the faucet just below the cupboard. He drinks a long, satisfying drink.

His glance falls on the plant again and he quickly fills the same glass with water and takes it to the window and waters the plant. He returns the glass to the sideboard, and to the immediate left of the window he selects a record and puts it on a turntable and we hear soft mood music after he places the arm on the record. He lifts his paper off the chair, sits, opens and reads his paper.

Mr. Right
Enters from USR and goes to the right door. He is carrying a large rectangular painting about 30 inches wide and 24 inches deep. He takes his keys from his pocket, opens the door and enters his apartment. He turns on the light switch to his immediate left on the imaginary wall. His nose does a little sniff at the staleness in the room. He places the painting

upright on the seat of the chair and goes to the window. He opens it up wide, pokes his head out and looks right and left and down and inhales a deep breath.

He stands back from the window and to his immediate right shapes by steadying a canary cage. He wiggles his fingers, does kisses with his lips and takes delight in reacting to his canary. He gets a thought and goes to the cupboard and fills a glass from the faucet. He returns to the cage, opens the little swing door with his right hand and retracts the water bath. He fills it from the glass and returns it to the cage shutting the swing door. He toasts the canary and drinks the balance of the water in his glass.

Placing the empty glass on the sideboard he lifts his painting using both hands and in an experimental fashion holds it up to gauge how it will look in various areas of the wall. He finally selects a position dead centre on the centre-stage wall. He places the picture on the chair again and goes to a drawer by the sink and gets a small nail and a hammer. He taps it into the wall.

Mr. Left

Hears the tapping and goes to the wall. As Mr. Right is returning the hammer to the drawer, he takes off his shoe and taps the nail back. He then returns to his chair and continues reading.

Mr. Right

Picks up his picture and attempts to slide it down the wall in order to engage the wire on the nail. He bends lower and lower until almost sitting on the floor. He stands and twisting his body to turn the picture out of his way he turns around and sees the nail lying on the floor.

He puts the picture back on the chair, lifts the nail and measures it between his index finger and thumb. A little shake of his head negates this nail. Back he goes to the open drawer, scattering things about looking for a larger nail. He finds a spike. It is at least five inches long, measured between his thumb and middle finger. He nods satisfaction to himself, takes the hammer, positions the spike and gives it a tremendous blow.

Mr. Left

Jumps out of his skin and watches in fascination as the nail protrudes through the wall into his apartment.

Mr. Right

Continues with three more blows to the nail. He turns and lifting the painting quickly hangs it on the spike and sits back on his chair to examine and appreciate it.

Mr. Left

Stands, throws his paper onto the chair. Strides to the door, swings it wide open and going to his neighbour's door, gives it three loud knocks.

Mr. Right

Much more interested in his new painting goes to the door and indifferently opens it and beckons to his neighbour to look at his beautiful painting as he re-sits.

Mr. Left

Comes in a pace and with arms on hips waits till he has Mr. Right's attention, then slowly beckons with his index finger "come with me" and returns to his apartment.

Mr. Right

With unconcern and a final look at his new work follows through the open doors.

Mr. Left

With a flourish of his DS arm, indicates the spike protruding through the wall.

Mr. Right

Gives a guilty little start with hand to mouth. He thinks for a moment. With a smile he indicates, "You just wait here, I know what to do." He quickly returns through the open doors to his apartment.

He takes the painting off the wall and with care he shuffles back and sideways through the doors and hangs the picture on the spike in Mr. Left's apartment. He pats Mr. Left a friendly pat on the back and indicates that the painting is now his.

Mr. Left

Smiling with astonishment, sits again and nods, "Hey, that's not bad, at all."

Mr. Right

Much pleased with himself, turns on his heel, goes back through his own door. In passing the nail in his wall, without thinking of the consequences, he just thinks to himself, "Oh, I won't be needing that nail now." He pulls it out and sits, and looks at his empty wall.

Mr. Left

Admiring the picture, jumps to his feet as it crashes to the floor. He does a slow "burn." With great control he bends and scoops up the debris. Awkwardly, he takes it into the next apartment and flings it to the floor and returns to his own chair to sit and fume.

Mr. Right

Astounded at this action, and not understanding, can only sit and watch the retreating back of his neighbour. Confused, he picks up the debris and with his toe, opens a garbage can and disposes of the broken piece of art. He begins to wonder, and quickly taking his chair, he places it under the nail hole, and very cautiously he peers through and sees his neighbour sitting and fuming across the room.

He gets an idea and with a sense of mischievousness he goes to the sideboard, fills the glass from the tap and takes a mouthful of water, his cheeks puffing out as he holds it in his mouth. He then gropes in the drawer again and finds a 12-inch straw which he shapes.

He tip-toes back to the chair and puts the straw through the nail hole and blows the water through. Quickly, he disposes of the straw in the receptacle and sits trying to maintain an innocent composure.

Mr. Left

Flays his arms trying to protect himself against the water and stands drenched down his front. He brushes it off. He takes his chair and places it below the nail hole and cautiously starts to position himself to see through.

Mr. Right

Not hearing a commotion, takes his chair again and looks through the hole. They see each other. Mr. Right dashes back to the original position with his chair.

Mr. Left

Looks around the room, sees his record player and gets an idea. He pulls the plug out of the wall which stops the music, and then pulls the other end out of the record player.

Mr. Right

Hearing the music stop, shrugs indifferently and leans over to the sideboard and turns on his mantle radio. There is perky music.

Mr. Left

Takes the extension cord and twists the bare wires of the one end and threads them through the nail hole and continues to push the wire through.

Mr. Right

With a double take, notices the wire start to come through the nail hole on his side of the wall and follows it with his head and eyes until it reaches the floor. He gets off his chair and, inquisitive, he picks up the bare wire and wonders to himself what is happening.

Mr. Left

Pauses with the prong end of the extension cord, poised near a low wall outlet. He plunges the connection in.

Mr. Right

Gets the full impact of the electrical current and his hand, arm and whole body begin to vibrate as he is frozen to the bare wire.

Mr. Left

Comes into the room to see how his joke is working. He sees Mr. Right shaking like mad. He points with arm extended and laughs.

Mr. Right

Grabs Mr. Left's extended hand and they both vibrate.

Mr. Left

Pulls Mr. Right back into his apartment, all the while shaking, and eventually is able to pull the plug and break the connection.

Mr. Right

They stand panting for a moment. Mr. Right looks around the room. He sees the potted flower and with a maniacal look goes to the window. He takes the plant and holds it out the window. Looking at Mr. Left, in glee he drops the plant and brushing off his hands he returns to his apartment.

Mr. Left

Stunned for a moment, quickly follows. He looks around Mr. Right's room and his glance rests on the canary. A look of insane murder comes over his face.

Mr. Right

Who has been watching Mr. Left, follows his gaze, sees his intention and hands in prayerful attitude, implores him, "Don't."

Mr. Left

Goes to the cage. He opens the hinge door and putting his hand in, he catches the bird and with both hands extracts it and takes it quickly to the window and releases it to freedom. He returns to his apartment and sits.

The Rhythm begins to quicken now.

Mr. Right

Follows, looks around the room. He goes to the record player, takes the record off the player, stoops and takes further records from the record cabinet below, stacking them in a pile on his left arm. Crossing to the window, he stands by the opening and one by one floats them out into space like frisbees, having a marvellous time.

Mr. Left

Watches the first couple fly out, and without waiting for the obvious, goes into the next apartment, immediately to the cupboard, opens it, and takes out a stack of good china plates. He goes to the open window and flings them out one by one in retaliation.

Mr. Right

Arrives on the scene just as he is finishing. He looks in the cupboard. Mr. Left has missed taking a plate. Mr. Right hands it to Mr. Left, who flings it out. Mr. Right burns and goes into Mr. Left's apartment, followed by Mr. Left. He goes directly to the record player, rips it out and pushes it out the window.

Mr. Left

Watching from his door, goes back to Mr. Right's apartment and pulls the radio off the wall. The music stops. He throws the radio out the window. He takes the canary cage and throws it out the window. He rolls up the carpet and throws it out the window.

Mr. Right

Still in Mr. Left's apartment, takes the scotch bottle, has a quick swig and throws it out the window. *He times it so that he is rolling up the carpet at the same time as Mr. Left, and they throw them out the respective windows in concert.*

They both look around the bare rooms. They notice the light bulbs, overhead, center. They take their chairs and standing on them together they unscrew the bulbs and throw them out of the respective windows, to a blackout.

A Duet

Vespers
Precis

Two monks, a senior and a novice, ring the steeple bells calling the others to Vespers.

The novice arrives in the tower first and, not fully impressed with the seriousness of his responsibilities and the importance of his work, shirks his duties, hiding from his senior. Eventually the senior, in a mildly reproving way, suggests the novice start ringing the bells.

He does so, but finds the bells emit no sound. They test each other's ropes. The novice cannot ring the bells but the senior can.

Inadvertently they bump each other and there is a tinkle. They test this out and find that the tinkle comes from the senior.

Realizing that the ability comes from within, the novice contritely prays for forgiveness. He is then able to ring the bells long and loud along with the senior.

Mimedrama

Players	**A senior monk, kindly, considerate, compassionate.**
	A novice monk, naive, simple, friendly.
Properties	**Sound effects, either live or on tape, of a full church bell and a little tinkling bell.**

(Entrances are made from behind a masking flat and are executed from a crouch, showing the arm first and simulating the climbing of steep stairs into the belfry.)

Novice

Enters as above from USL and comes to DSR. He looks up into the steeple, gives a sigh of weariness as if there must be many more interesting things to be done. He is about to reach up for the imaginary rope when he hears something. He looks sharply up to the entrance, then goes USL and looks down the steep stairwell. He sees the senior monk climbing and quickly flattens himself hiding against the stairwell wall.

Monk

Enters as above, very tired. He looks back down the stairwell as if to say: "It is getting steeper every day." He turns and goes to DSC to an imaginary devotional area. He kneels, crosses himself, and prays a short prayer. With difficulty he rises and prepares to go to his rope, which is DSL.

Novice

Who has been repressing his giggles with difficulty, gradually realizes the deep devotion of the senior monk. He is drawn further DS and SL of the senior monk.

Monk

Now notices the novice and stops in his tracks. With a small smile of understanding he looks back and up to the novice's bell rope SR, then quizzically and with a look of anticipation back to the novice.

Novice

Returns a quick look of puzzlement. Then, with a start and a great deal more understanding, he crosses US of the monk in a contrite manner, head bowed. Apologetically, he crosses over to SR and stands under his bell rope. He makes a great show of rolling up his sleeves in preparation for the important work he now realizes he must do.

Monk

Satisfied that his little helper is about to do his job, reaches up and pulls his bell rope. (A *"clang-a-clang" lovely ringing is heard.*)

Novice

About to ring his bell, sees the monk start to pull the rope and is drawn to watch the master.

Monk

Busily ringing his bell, becomes aware that the novice is taking an unduly long time. He stops pulling his own rope and looks reproachfully at the novice.

Novice

With a start, realizes he has not been doing his duty, and reaches up to grip his bell rope. With a great flourish he pulls it down, but there is no sound. He stops, looks up into the steeple, and pulls the rope again. There is no sound. He stops and looks enquiringly at the monk.

Monk

Responds and moves into the novice's area as the novice backs off and around to CS to give him room. He pulls the novice's bell rope, producing a lovely "clang-a-clang" of the bells, and then stops.

Novice

Goes to the senior monk's bell rope and confidently gives it a mighty pull. Nothing. He stops and looks at the monk who comes over. Both look up into the steeple. The novice shakes the rope. They bend back and inadvertently bump shoulders. (*There is a "tinkle-tinkle" sound.*)

Startled, they stand back from each other. The novice is curious and with his forefinger he pokes his own chest. Nothing. With reverent anticipation, he points his finger at the monk's chest and pokes him. (*There is a "tinkle-tinkle" sound.*)

With sudden comprehension he looks to the devotional area and quickly goes DSC, kneels, closes his eyes, and clasps his hand to his lips in an attitude of prayer. Shaking his head to underline his seriousness, the novice points his left thumb to SL, then shakes his head. His right thumb points to SR and again he shakes his head. His prayer is apparently complete and he is about to rise when some premonition causes him to look back to the watching monk.

Monk

Cants his head reproachfully.

Novice

Quickly crosses himself and then rises. With pleasant anticipation he goes to his own bell SR. He prepares to pull it and, with a slight nod from the senior monk, he does so, producing a lovely "clang-a-clang" sound. The pulls become stronger and stronger, and eventually his feet are being pulled up off the belfry floor.

Monk

Watches for a few moments, and then begins to pull his bell rope. The two monks alternately pull their bell ropes and a lovely mingling of bell sounds is heard, calling the other monks to vespers as the lights fade to black.

Territorial Rights

Précis

A very young person has established an unwritten claim to a park bench. Finding an intruder using the bench, the young person can only use an accusative stare as a weapon. The intruder tries several ways of establishing a rapport with the child, but is continuously met with the stare, to a point where there is no delight left for the intruder who leaves. The child reaffirms his territorial right.

Mimedrama

Players	A little girl (can be a boy)
	The Stroller: Average, open, warm
Properties	A bench, CS
	A litter basket
	A ball

Child

Discovered lying on her back on the bench, head supported by US arm, legs crossed in the air. The foot of the dangling leg beats rhythm each time she lightly tosses a real ball up and catches it again. *Toss, catch. Toss, catch.* Bored with this she sits up and taps her heels against the bench. Bored with this, she goes to one end of the bench and starts the ball on a slow roll while she runs to the other end and catches the ball as it rolls off. Repeat this to the other end. She paces off two steps from one end of the bench, bends over, aims and rolls the ball through her legs to strike bench end. Recovers ball, paces off three steps and repeats. Paces off four steps and this time the ball misses and rolls into the wings SR. She chases after it.

Stroller

Strolls on from SL just as child runs off. Glances around and reacts to the warm sun appreciating the lovely day and the setting. Sits on the bench and takes imaginary apple from pocket.

Child

Re-enters and stops suddenly as she sees the stroller sitting on HER bench. She stops slightly US and a few paces R and stares.

Stroller

Makes quite a business of polishing the apple, and just as he is about to relish a bit, suddenly stops with mouth half open, intuitively aware that all is not well. As he feels the eyes boring into the back of his neck he slowly turns his head until he meets the child's eyes. They stare blankly at each other for three beats. He turns back to the apple which has been held fixed point, ready to be eaten, smiles, misinterpreting the child's stare as a desire for the apple.

child
Moves DS so that she is even with, and closer to, the stroller.

Stroller
Turns suddenly to offer apple at arms length to the child.

Child
Startled at sudden motion, draws back a half pace and continues to stare deadpan at stroller.

Stroller
Reinforces his offer of the apple with a further hand motion and a larger smile.

Child
Stands motionless with a deadpan stare, not reacting.

Stroller
Slightly annoyed that his winning personality hasn't won over the child, turns slowly front, withdrawing his offering and staring at the apple. We see an idea register as a slight smile on his face, and he goes into an exaggerated act of taking a bit of the apple and overly reacting to the delicious taste, closing his eyes, literally drooling over the apple.

Child
Without taking her eyes off him, crosses quickly US behind him and down to the other side of the bench.

Stroller
Assuming that his "acting" has given the child a desire for the apple, suddenly drops his "act" and offers the apple to his right, where the child had been. Noticing that she is not there, he assumes that she has left and looks off R after her. He gives a sigh of relief as he turns back to the apple, smiling in anticipation. He takes a bite and is chewing happily when suddenly he stops. The thought just struck him that he hasn't checked SL. With trepidation he slowly turns his head, confirms his fear and snaps his head back front.

Child
Remains immobile, simply staring.

Stroller
Slowly begins to chew again with determination, anger building rapidly within him. Suddenly, he stands to face the child.

Child
Once again, startled by the suddenness of the move, backs up a quick little step and stares.

Stroller
Following up on his advantage, takes a quick step toward her.

Child
Backs up a pace.

Stroller
Stamps his feet in quick succession as one might shoo home a little dog.

Child
Turns quickly and runs OSL.

Stroller
Gives gesture of "good riddance" and steps back to bench area and proceeds to sit.

Child
Returns in an abrupt entrance the moment the stroller's seat meets the bench.

Stroller
Senses that the brat has returned and freezes for just a beat, as an after beat on the child's re-entrance. However, he continues to sit and in an overly-relaxed manner makes a show of enjoying the last three bites of the apple. Underneath this pretence we can really see that the child's presence is getting to him and builds to a point when he stands and throws the apple core to the ground in anger and exits SR without looking at the child, throwing his arms up in exasperation, his stroll ruined.

Child
Follows his exit a couple of paces to SR. Still with deadpan expression returns to pick up apple core and throw it in litter basket, then sits, looking out front for a beat. Slowly a beautiful all-knowing smile breaks on her face and she lies back as in the opening attitude, tossing the ball and beating time with her crossed leg as the lights fade to black.

A Trio

The Hole

Precis

Based on an animated Disney cartoon.

A public utilities foreman and his helper arrive and establish a hole in the ground by literally placing a representational hole, either a circle or a circular cut-out, on the floor. They are proud of their hole and one of them goes down into it.

A passerby notices this. The workman returns and the foreman, on seeing the rapture of his subordinate, decides to go down. He returns and the two relate their great experience to each other.

The passerby, intrigued, jumps down the hole. The workmen look around for the passerby and not seeing him they take their hole and leave.

Mime Drama

Players	A Public Utilities Foreman His Helper A Passerby
Properties	A black circular piece of canvas or a rectangular piece of black canvas with a circle cut out. In either case, the circle is approximately one metre in diameter. It is carried rolled up in the form. The foreman carries an imaginary coil of rope.

Foreman
Enters from USR and comes down stage and around and back to USR looking for a suitable place to dig a hole. He places the coil of rope DSR.

Helper
Enters from USR and crosses directly and exits USL. He carries the hole rolled up and over his shoulder.

Foreman
Notices him exiting and dashes US with hand and arm raised in a hailing attitude, beckoning him to come back.

Helper
Returns and comes down to his boss with a simple, but eager-to-help attitude.

Foreman
Points DSL.

Helper
Is about to lay the hole down.

Foreman
Stops him with a hand gesture and points to a spot USR.

Helper
Eager to please, scampers US and is about to lay out the hole.

Foreman

Once again stops him and points to the original DSL spot.

Helper

Raises his eyes heavenward. "After all!" Anticipating that the boss will change his mind again, he waits, enjoying the scenery.

Foreman

Notices his helper goofing off. He puts both fists on his hips and glares at his apprentice.

Helper

Still preoccupied with the beautiful spot, notices with a double take, that his boss is looking at him. For a brief moment he returns the look, naively, with a blank friendly smile.

Foreman

Exasperated, stamps his foot, and points to the DSL spot.

Helper

Understanding, jumps to obey. He places the hole just on stage US of the DSL leg. (*In black out, those who are using the hole can easily jump off stage unseen by the audience.*) He stands back and with a big smile looks to the boss for approbation.

Foreman

Does a circular move around the hole musing and judging its perfection.

Helper

Follows, imitating the boss' mannerisms. They end where they started.

Foreman

Kneels on one knee to peer down the hole better.

Helper

Watches. He gets an idea and steps right a pace to pick up a stone. He raises it and is obviously going to drop it.

Foreman

Without looking at his helper puts his right hand out, obviously demanding the stone.

Helper

Drops the stone onto the foreman's hand.

Foreman

Holds the stone over the hole and drops it. They both listen in anticipation as three slow beats go by. Still nothing.

Slowly the boss looks at his helper in amazement. How deep is the hole? At this precise moment, they both react to what seems to have been a terrific explosion. The boss puts his finger in his ear as if to clear it of water.

They both kneel and peer down this amazing hole.

Helper

Getting an idea, cups his hands as if to yell down the hole.

Foreman

With a restraining gesture, takes over this further testing of their hole. He cups his hands and mimes a double yell "yoo hoo" down the well.

They both listen in anticipation for about three beats. Then the foreman indicates by a conducting gesture that, away in the distance, they hear the two beats of the faint "yoo hoo."

Getting to his feet, the foreman looks at his helper with a very self-satisfied look and nods his head in approval.

Helper

Rises to his feet, beaming a broad smile and looking directly back at his boss.

Foreman

Looking directly at his helper, gestures to him to jump down the hole.

Helper

Holds the look for a beat or so. Then slowly, to confirm that he understands the invitation, points to himself, then to the hole, followed by a mini-gesture of diving into it.

Foreman

Nods his head twice, slowly, in affirmation.

Helper

Now that this horrendous invitation has been confirmed, quickly refuses with a shake of his head followed by a magnanimous gesture of invitation to the boss. After all, the boss always goes first.

From L to R; Adrian Pecknold, Harro Maskow and Wayne Specht from the Canadian Mime Theatre, performing in *The Hole*.

Foreman
His assurance shaken, once again he kneels at the left side of the hole and, looking down, gives the situation more serious thought.

Passerby
Crosses from USL to USR quickly and purposefully. He sees the two workmen peering down the hole. His curiosity is piqued. He slows his pace considerably and comes DSR. He leans in the direction of the two men until he realizes that the foreman has caught him "nosing" in. He looks guiltily away, and pretends he is just waiting around.

Foreman
Nudges his helper, rises, and indicates the new arrival with a cant of his head. He gets the passerby's attention and invites him to look down their hole.

Passerby
Pleased at this act of friendliness, comes quickly to the onstage side of the hole and peers down. He examines it intently and admiringly for a few beats, then straightens and, turning to the two workmen, nods his head in an attitude of "Wow! That's quite a hole you've got there."

Foreman
Agrees, and very broadly invites him to jump down the hole.

Passerby
Looks first at the foreman, then at the helper, shakes his head in disbelief and moves several paces back to SR. He is thinking these guys must be out of their minds to suggest such a thing. He folds his arms in justifiable determination.

Foreman

Crosses slowly to the passerby's left. They look dead-pan at each other for a beat.

The foreman beckons with his head, looking over his shoulder, smiling broadly, and repeating his invitation.

Passerby

Smiles broadly in response, but quickly shakes his head. "Not on your life." He notices the helper.

Helper

Has been standing quite still near the hole. As the foreman offers the second invitation, he supports the offer by acting out the various methods the passerby might employ if he agrees to dive down the hole.

He might do a high dive; he runs his fingers along his forearm to the elbow and, with his hand, executes a beautiful high dive into the well. Or he might do a two-and-a-half gainer; he puts his hands together in a diving attitude and follows it with a rapid rotation of one hand around the other and into the hole. He is carried away with his own suggestions and continues to jump up and down.

Passerby

Has noticed these peculiar antics and nods to the foreman that he should look at his helper. They both do.

Helper

Becomes aware that the others are staring at him and slowly stops his movements, self-consciously scuffing his toe on the ground in embarrassment.

Foreman

Exchanges a look with the passerby and crosses back to the helper. Once again he nods with his head a gesture of "Go on, jump."

Helper

Looking miserably uncomfortable, prepares to jump. Drawing back, he implores his boss "Please, don't make me." (His heart wasn't in it, at all.)

Foreman

With an authoritative gesture, orders the helper to jump down the hole.

Helper

Gives a preparatory caution by adopting a diving attitude, in order that the stage manager or lighting man will know the exact lighting cue. He jumps up. (*The lights fade to a quick blackout.*) The actor gets quickly off SL behind the leg and waits, out of sight, for his next cue. (*The lights come up again.*)

Foreman

Is sitting bored and dozing near the hole. They have been waiting for a considerable time.

Passerby

Is sitting a pace or two to the right of the hole. He checks his watch. Hearing a sound, he motions to the foreman to do something.

Foreman

Bounds to his feet and points to the coil of rope that he curled SR at the beginning of the sketch.

Passerby

Quickly gets the rope and tosses one end to the foreman. They let it down into the hole, hand-over-hand, and brace themselves to pull up the helper. They pull up the rope, hand-over-hand, for four pulls. (*The lights fade to black.*) For the fifth pull they wait in blackout. (*The lights come back up.*)

Helper

As soon as the lights are black, gets on stage as if he has just reached the top edge of the well.

Passerby

Pulls with the foreman and, on the fifth and subsequent pulls, they help the helper out. The passerby winds up the rope over his hand and elbow and puts the coil back in its original place.

Foreman

Who had untied the rope from around the waist of his helper now stands looking at him.

Helper

Stands loose and relaxed, smiling beatifically, as one who has experienced something marvelous.

Passerby

Looks at the helper, then at the foreman, and they both go rapidly to the hole and look down.

They look again to the helper and then at each other.

Foreman
Gestures with his head. "Do you want to try it?"

Passerby
Thinks about it for a brief moment, then suggests with his hand "You?"

Foreman
Makes a decision, points and nods, "O.K. get me the rope."

Passerby
Quickly gets the rope and tosses one end to the foreman.

Foreman
Ties it off around his waist.

Passerby
Being ready, gives the helper a punch on the arm nodding to the rope "Come on, give a hand."

Helper
Still spaced-out, lifts the rope between the passerby and the foreman and stands in a trance.

Foreman
Standing at the mouth of the hole preparing to jump, again notices the look on the helper's face. He gives the rope a little pull. The passerby and the helper allow their hands to respond to the foreman's pull on the imaginary rope. Satisfied that everything is ready, he jumps. The lights fade to black, and the foreman exits quickly to behind the DSL leg.

Helper
Feeds the rope out rapidly as the foreman goes down.

Passerby
Taking visual cues from the helper, he also feeds the rope out as the lights go to black. Lights come up and we find the helper and the passerby waiting.

Helper
Still a little spaced-out, is holding the rope much as an angler would hold a fishing line.

His hand responds to what might be described as a nibble on the line. There is a much bigger series of pulls.

Passerby
Gives the helper a poke to wake him up and they get into position to pull up the rope. Once again they pull four times as the lights go to black.

Foreman
As was done before, positions himself as if climbing over the mouth of the hole and the lights come on.

Helper
Again finishes pulling the rope up and unties it from around the foreman's waist. He is looking in eager anticipation into the face of the foreman.

Foreman
Has the same "full of awe" look as the helper. They put their arms around each others' shoulders and turn US away from the hole, as if to compare notes, and stand in tableau.

Passerby
As before, goes quickly to the hole and peers down into it to see what is having this exceptional effect on the utility men. He notices that they are not watching him, and he decides to pluck up his courage and dive in. He jumps up, then quickly exits offstage, as the lights go to black.

Foreman
The lights come up and we find the helper and foreman still in the attitude we left them. They break tableau and turn down stage as if to tell the passerby of their experience.

He is not there. They look off into the wings but still can't find him. They double check opposite sides.

No luck. "Oh well," shrugs the foreman. "Let's go." He points to the hole. He picks up and winds his coil of rope.

Helper
Picks up the hole and rolls it up, placing it over his shoulder. They exit very rapidly.

(Blackout.)

The Chiropractor

Précis

A doctor of chiropractic and his apprentice work on a client in dire straights. They beat him and pummel him, knead and ply him until he is feeling quite relaxed and limber. In saying good bye they slap him on the back and his muscles retract in the original fashion.

Mimedrama

Players	Doctor of Chiropractic
	Novice Apprentice
	A Patient Client
Properties	a massage table in the centre of the room

Doctor
Discovered on stage with his apprentice he flexes his knees in a little jerk and pulls his arms back in a habitual little ritual he does whenever he is about to use his artistry or whenever he thinks on the move. He follows this with a quick little wiggle of his fingers to reassure himself they are working.

Novice
Convinced that this ritual is an integral part of chiropractic methods, he emulates his master. Every time the Doctor flexes, he follows suit. he also dogs his masters footsteps, always at one side or another.

Doctor
Flexes his muscles and walks around the table. He straightens the DSL corner of the cloth cover. He ends USC of the table.

Novice
Following the Doctor, he repeats and copies everything the Doctor does ending US at the Doctors right and completing the cross with the muscle flexing ritual as the Doctor has done.

There is a knock on the door USL.

Doctor
Takes a step back, flexes his muscles and indicates to admit the patient.

Novice
Repeats the ritual. Crosses DS of the doctor and stops. He turns and relates to the Doctor (who nods his approval). All of a sudden the novice goes wild with the flexing ritual, completely out of control he goes into a spastic fit.

Doctor

Quickly taps him on the head and gives a cautionary wag, 'now, now' with his finger.

Novice

Stops, dead pan. Having regained his composure he opens the door and with his on-stage hand (right) gestures the patient to come in.

Patient

Enters with his head canted at a severe angle to his left. his right arm has stiffened from the shoulder to the elbow horizontal to the floor. The forearm dangles uselessly. He wears a self pitying look and winces in pain at the slightest touch. He stops between the Doctor and the Novice and looks out to the audience.

Doctor

Gives the patient's arm a squeeze.

Patient

Winces in pain and comes DSL a little to clear the sight lines.

Novice

Stops the patient in a reassuring manner.

Doctor

Comes down to the patient and reassures him. He flexes, he takes the patients head and slowly rocks it first right then left, right, left and finally a quick snap right. (An off-stage sound by a toy ratchet sounds great.)

Patient

Freezes with a grimace of pain. Slowly a smile of realization spreads over his face. His right arm is still rigidly at right angles to the floor. He moves his head from side to side, very pleased. He looks sorrowfully at his arm and then to the Doctor, questioningly.

Doctor

Smiles knowingly. He flexes for effect. (The novice copies as always.) He goes a little US of the patient and placing his left hand on the patient's right shoulder, he suddenly pushes the patient's elbow down with his right hand.

Patient

Allows his right arm to go down and stay down, but strangely and as if they were joined together, his left leg bends up at the knee and stays there.

Novice

Looks at the Doctor, who nods his head. He flexes like his master. He raises his right hand and gives the patient a sharp slap on the knee.

Patient

As his leg goes down, his arm goes back up. This is repeated, each time a little faster.

Doctor

On fourth try, holds the arm down.

Patient

On fourth try, leaves the leg down.

Novice

Anticipating, on the fourth try drops on his stomach to the floor and tackles the patient's legs, holding them tight. He waits a beat and then carefully and slowly he releases the legs and gets to his feet.

Doctor

Carefully releases the patient's arm and stands back a pace.

Patient

Undulates his arm slowly. Very pleased he tests his neck and head, his arms, his legs, etc.

Doctor

During this, physically leads the patient to an USC position behind the chiropractic table. When in position he pretends to take the patient's hair and lift.

Novice

Who has followed, pretends to take the seat of the patient's pants and lift.

Patient

In reality, springs up and lands face down on the table in coordination with the actions of the Doctor and the Novice.

Doctor

Roughly turns the patient over.

Patient

Sits up.

Doctor

Pushes the patient's upper body down again.

Patient

Legs come up together at right angles.

Novice

Pulls them down. This happens three times. Then the Doctor and Novice start the two-hand-chop massage.

Doctor

Starting at the head, chops along the patient from the DS side of the table.

Novice

Starting at the feet, chops along the US side of the table.

Doctor

When he reaches the feet, he goes to the end of the table, takes the patient's legs and swings them.

Patient

Sitting partly up at this point, allows his whole body to turn on his seat so that he is now laying in the opposite direction.

Doctor

Continues to chop slap the patient on the US side, back to his feet again.

Novice

Repeats on the DS side.

Patient

During all this has responded with a greatly exaggerated vibration of his total body. The massage ends. The Doctor and Novice are spar-flexing at either end of the table. He lies still for a beat and then cautiously sits up. His legs are dangling over the table. He feels his knees, then his elbows and biceps muscles. He feels and turns his head. He gets off the table and for a moment his legs go to jelly, but he recovers to stand pleased, very aware of his new body DSC.

Doctor

And the Novice make a false start to support the patient when he first gets off the table. However, he doesn't need help. They both come DS to stand on either side of him. Together they give the patient a friendly slap on the back, and stand back a pace.

Patient

The arm snaps back to its original affliction, at the same time the head snaps back and freezes to its original quirk. He stands this way for a beat.

Doctor and Novice

Looking at the patient, turn their heads slowly to the audience and as the lights fade their hands spread in a *"C'est la vie"* fashion, as the sketch ends in black.

A Quartet

Doctor's Waiting Room

Précis

Four patients arrive one at a time to await their appointment.

A young, flushed mother-to-be, delighted with her condition.

A miserable person with an atrocious spastic tick which periodically and uncontrollably pulls the left side of his face out of shape.

A person whose left leg is in a cast from hip to foot.

A fourth person with a skin irritation covering his whole body. Only his embarrassment prevents him from scratching.

Several instances of contact between the patients results in a sympathetic spread of the itchy feeling to all the characters.

Mimedrama

Players	Expectant Mother	Her first child.
	Twitchy	Nervous tick spasm left side of face.
	Gimpy	Left leg completely encased in cast.
	Itchy	Allergy affecting total body.
Properties	Four stools or boxes spread across stage, the fourth DS of the other three. Also DS, the door to the office.	

Mother

Enters two steps USR, weight on heels, abdomen grossly distended. She is in an imaginary corridor running from USR to DSR. She pauses briefly and as she turns to come downstage her right hand rests for a moment on her abdomen and we see an expression of beatitude on her face as she contemplates the marvellous natural approach to child birth the doctor has been teaching her.

She turns to face an imaginary DS door and despite a little trouble in seeing the imaginary doorknob, throws the door open onstage and steps into the waiting room, gently pushing the door closed behind her. She glances slowly around this beautiful, beautiful room where she has been coming to wait each week for the past eight and a half months. There are no others here and her favorite chair, number three near the magazine table, is free.

She half backs toward the chair reaching out with her left arm to feel for it, and supporting her abdomen with her right hand, she slowly eases herself down to sit on the chair, letting her breath out in relief as she feels the comfort of taking the weight off her feet.

She glances down to her left and notices a new babyfood magazine. She picks it up, thumbs through it, props it partly on her stomach and contentedly reads a beautiful article on pablum.

Twitchy

Enters two paces on stage from USR, and, as he turns to come down the hall, the whole left side of his face contracts in a dreadful spastic spasm. He looks terribly sad and unhappy, because this nervous tick has been recurring every minute or so uncontrollably since early morning.

He turns and enters the waiting room through imaginary DSR door and slips unnoticed into the seat to the right of the mother, feeling miserable and looking straight out front.

Mother

Aware that someone has sat down beside her, slowly turns with a large warm welcoming smile.

Twitchy

Unable to control his face, gives a terrible twitch just at that moment.

Mother

Startled, turns away, no longer smiling. She cannot believe her eyes, and thoughts of her beautiful child being marked for life cross her mind. Slowly unable to resist, she turns to check again.

Twitchy

Wanting to smile assurance but unable to control his spasms, twitches again and turns from her, looking even more miserable.

Mother

Her worst fears confirmed, in rapid succession hides, with her magazine as a shield, first her face, then her abdomen. Finally she labouriously shifts from her chair to the fourth DS chair and tries to protect her body by hiding behind, and pretending to read, the magazine.

Gimpy

Limps, or rather throws the weight of his heavy straight leg on stage and comes down to the door. He is smoking, takes a last drag and throws the butt to the floor as he is about to enter. Realizing the fire hazard he turns back to the smouldering butt and swings his stiff cast to stub it out. He reaches for the door handle and throws the door open into the room. He swings his leg through and hops in on his good leg until he clears the door which he then slams. The seat number three seems easiest for him and he limps and hops to the chair. He slowly eases onto the chair and, as he takes the weight on his good leg, his cast leg snaps up to the horizontal and he settles for a moment.

He notices the mother and, particularly, the cover of her magazine showing a beautiful blond baby with pablum all over its face. He points to the cover and turns in a spirit of camaraderie to Twitchy. With a large smile on his face, he is about to remark on the humorous portrait.

Twitchy

Once again, not being in control under the tension of this pending contact, twitches.

Gimpy

Forgetting what his repartee was going to be, turns front with his smile frozen on his face. Gradually the smile dissolves and matches the puzzled look in his eyes, and he turns slowly back to check out this weird reaction.

Twitchy

At this point gives the worst twitch of the day and turns front in absolute helplessness.

Gimpy

Mesmerized, glues his eyes on this strange character. His stiff leg involuntarily swings left onto the lap of the prospective mother and has hit her abdomen.

Mother

Absorbed in magazine, thinks for a minute that this is the strongest kick she has yet felt from her child. Her hand goes to her abdomen and finds Gimpy's ankle. She becomes aware of what has happened and in simmering outrage, replaces the magazine with one hand and thrusts Gimpy's cast away with the other. She rises as the cast swings back to rest on the seat she is vacating, and she makes her way to seat number one to the right of Twitchy. She sits and, slowly, she and Gimpy lean forward to take a better look at each other.

Twitchy
At this moment, not able to stand double scrutiny, twitches twice out front, then, cupping clasped hands between his knees, looks devastated. All three sit quietly.

Itchy
Enters USR. He is excrutiatingly itchy. His fingernails are clenched into the palms of each hand. From childhood illnesses he remembers the caution not to scratch. Somehow he feels dirty and unclean and embarrassed. He tries not to scratch, but would love to tear his skin off. As he comes down to the floor, he allows himself a wrist on wrist scratch, then he quickly tackles the back of his head and a spot below his right eye. Then he recovers his willpower and prepares to enter.

Just as he thinks he is ready, he weakens, gives the small of his back a brief but indulgent scratch, then quickly composes himself and enters, hoping there are no other patients in the waiting room.

As he enters, all together look up at him. He freezes for a moment, beating down the urge to flee. He gathers his courage, closes the door, then realizes the only vacant seat is across the room and Gimpy is using it for a foot-stool.

Slowly he crosses, resisting the urge to scratch, particularly as every head in the waiting room turns in concert, watching his every move.

He arrives a little DSL of the vacant chair, and keeping his back away from them, he allows his right hand a vigorous quick scratch to his rear, recovers and continues a complete turn on the spot, now looking a little offstage DL as if hoping for another chair to materialize in order that he needn't impose or intrude on Gimpy's comfort.

He turns back and, almost apologetically, indicates to Gimpy that his leg is taking up a chair.

Gimpy
Comes out of his fascinated stare with a little start and swings his leg off the stool, still horizontal.

Itchy
Smiles an embarrassed acknowledgement and sits facing front, feigning composure, the others watching him as if mesmerized.

A look of absolute contained agony shows on his face, he bites his lip to refrain from scratching, his body tightens overly erect as an irresistible desire to scratch his right ankle comes over him. He attempts to scratch it with his left toe. This is not too satisfactory; he quickly crosses his right leg over his left knee and looks up at ceiling right, innocently attempting to divert the attention of the other three who can't take their eyes off him.

He slowly creeps his left hand down his leg to the itchy ankle and starts to scratch. He quickly closes his eyes in the relief of the moment and luxuriates in scratching the spot.

Suddenly he stops as his eyes open front, and he wonders if they have been and are still watching him. He throws a quick look, then flustered, uncrosses his legs and adopts as unconcerned a pose as possible.

The Three
Startled at Itchy's direct look at them, guiltily, all look away. Then each is drawn back to look at this person who acts so oddly.

Itchy
Tries unobtrusively to sneak a scratch here and there with his index finger and even his little finger on his upper lip and nose as if this etiquette might be acceptable.

Gimpy
Fascinated, leans forward, and still unable to take his eyes off Itchy, unconsciously scratches his own ankle and then stops.

Twitchy
Fascinated, very slowly allows his hand to go to to his knee and subconsciously he scratches, still watching Itchy.

Mother

Fascinated, unable to take her eyes off Itchy, finds her left hand scratching her right side as if she had on an itchy maternity girdle.

Itchy

The chain reaction ripples down the line once again, a little more rapidly through Gimpy, Twitchy and Mother, until they all realize that everyone is itching and begin to assist each other, and scratch themselves at the same time, ending as follows.

Mother

Scratching her midriff with her right hand and Twitchy's shoulder with her left.

From L to R; Robin Patterson, Harro Maskow, Ian Mackay, Adrian Pecknold of the Canadian Mime Theatre in *The Doctor's Waiting Room*. Originally performed at Niagara-on-the-Lake.

Twitchy

Stands in order to guide Mother's hand lower to his back at same time scratching Gimpy's back with both hands.

Gimpy

Offers to do Itchy's back and points with his hand to scratch his ankle.

Itchy

Responds by standing and rubbing his own itchy ankle with the cast on Gimpy's ankle.

(Lights fade to black.)

A Quartet

The Keystone Cops

Précis

A tribute to the silent screen era and the beautifully comedic, jerky, frame-by-frame technology of the early cameras. Many different scenarios can be conceived using a strobe light to simulate the technology of the day. Chase music should be played throughout.

Two keystone cops are guarding the National Bank. The beautiful secretary arrives to open up the bank. The bank robber sneaks out unseen by the cops. The secretary comes out to scream the alarm, a typical Keystone chase ensues and, of course, the robber is eventually caught, and justice prevails.

Mimedrama

Players	Cop 1	Dressed in full Bobby regalia including white gloves, billystick and belt and a black and white Bobby hat.
	Cop 2	Exactly the same.
	Girl	In a white flapper dress, she seems always ready to break out into a Charleston.
	Robber	Affecting a black mask over his eyes and a black and white fedora.
Costumes		Clichés, black and white to reflect the strobe light.
Properties		Strobe lights and chase music, starting simultaneously as the drama begins.

Cop 1
SL at attention, his billy stick twirling in a circle from his white-gloved hands, his belt and Bobby hat reflect the strobe light.

Cop 2
SR about three paces, completing the suggestion of the front entrance to the bank. He is doing exactly as Cop 1.

Girl
Enters from DSR, almost dancing the Charleston, goes into the bank by walking between the two cops, and exits USL.

Cops 1 & 2
Turn on their heels, batons twirling, and parade back and forth in front of the entrance to the bank.

Robber

On their third pass, when the cops' backs are to him, enters from USL (from inside the bank), carrying a white bag with a "$" painted on it. He sneaks off, exiting SR as the cop is doing a turn.

Girl

Enters from USL. She gesticulates and points left and right.

Cops 1 & 2

Come CS to the girl. They instruct each other to go in opposite directions and Cop 1 starts off SL while Cop 2 goes SR.

Robber

Enters from DSR crossing to DSL in front of the girl who remained on stage.

Cop 2

Enters from DSR, following the robber.

Girl

Points to the exit the robber has taken.

Cop 1

Enters from USL.

Girl

Points to the DSL exit and follows Cop 1 off who in turn is following Cop 2 who is following the robber.

(There now follows a series of crosses.)

From USL to DSR. Robber, followed by Cop 2, followed by Cop 1, followed by girl. All running with legs and arms going very fast but with little lateral progression.

Off stage, Cop 2 and 1 pass robber and enter from DSR in very high-stepping, very elongated running motion. They are followed by the robber, followed by the Girl.

Cop 2 continues quickly off stage, and crosses over to SR out of sight of the audience. Robber and Cop 2 now enter simultaneously from opposite sides. They turn with their backs to each other and start to exit.

Cop 1 enters from USL and stands between them. He taps Cop 2 on the shoulder and points to the robber exiting SR. Cop 2 turns, anticipating the robber, and hits Cop 1 on the helmet. Cop 1 spins and falls to the floor with a great flourish. Cop 2 goes to his assistance and picks him up. Cop 1 shakes off Cop 2 and goes into a tantrum of stamping feet, pointing to SR after the robber. Girl enters from USL and stops their argument. She points off SR and the chase resumes: Cop 1, Cop 2, girl.

The moment they exit SR, the robber enters from USR and comes down to CS. Elated, he does a few high jumps and side kicks. Cops 1 and 2 enter from USR and come down on either side of the robber. They both, at the same time, hit him on his fedora. The robber, his knees turned to rubber, oozes to a kneel. The cops hold their batons to "attention," grasping the robber with their inside hands. The girl runs to CS and holds, over the Robber's head, a black sign with white lettering: "The End." *(End of the music and blackout.)*

In principle, the stage should never be vacant for more than an instant. Big moves are far more effective under the strobe than small moves. Variations, slow to fast, are especially interesting. The possibilities are endless.

Any Number

The Audience

Précis

This has always been a good exercise to explore character relationships, actions, reactions and inter-actions between people.

A group of people comes, *en masse* or singly, into a movie theatre. The audience will come to know the actors quite well by watching them watching the movie and dealing with the interruptions that occur from time to time.

Set up a number of seats or boxes across the stage in one or more rows to simulate theatre seats.

A musical theme introduces the sketch (and thus the movie) and discreetly fades to silence. Similarly, the final credits can be indicated by the sudden introduction of the theme, which covers the exits.

Mimedrama

Players		
	Sleepy	Has a severe head cold, has been taking cold medicine with the result that he is very sleepy.
	Pa	A mild-mannered, middle-aged man in a bowler.
	Ma	An organizer with a motherly bent.
	A Lady of the Night	Very dated and somewhat long in the tooth, dressed to kill in a white feather boa and a floppy-brimmed hat.
	Masher	Sports a thin black moustache and a fedora that could have been worn by Al Capone.

Five boxes are set equidistant across the stage DS. There is an imaginary aisle down each side. The entrance is from USC. All entrances are made in the insecure, hesitant manner we can all remember when there is no usher to show us to a seat in the darkness.

Sleepy

Enters and comes down aisle SL. He is mesmerized by every action in a movie, even a B movie.

Keeping his eyes on the screen, supposedly straight out over the heads of the audience, i.e. the real audience, he reaches just the right row of seats and gropes his way to the centre seat and sits. He sniffs with the left nostril then the right, bending his nose out of shape to help block off the one as he sniffs with the other. Even so, he settles and drops his mouth open as the nostrils are still clogged.

Ma & Pa

Enter, Pa proceeding slowly down the aisle, pushed and prodded by Ma.

Pa is about to walk into the orchestra pit, when Ma decides they are close enough. Ma grabs him by the coat tail just before he takes the final fatal step; pulling him back to the row of seats and pushing him across the aisle. Like most people, Pa is watching the action on the screen and tries to sit in Sleepy's lap. Ma and Pa eventually sit and settle in to watch the film.

Ma is about to make a comment to Pa when she sees that he is still wearing a hat. Ma gives Pa a sharp little jab with her elbow and stares at his head. Pa turns his head slowly to Ma, a little annoyed at being disturbed, and is about to turn back to the movie when he sees the look of annoyance on *her* face. He comprehends and removes his hat.

Pa sits for a beat, then, deciding that if she wants him to take off his hat then she can hold it, thrusts it in front of her, all the while keeping his eyes on the screen. Ma takes the hat automatically and holds it on her lap.

Canadian Mime Theatre production of *The Audience*. L to R; Paulette Hallich, Ian Mackay, Adrian Pecknold, Harro Maskow, Robin Patterson.

Lady

Walks down the SR aisle in undulating fashion, looking for an empty seat next to a likely male prospect. She spots Sleepy.

A knowing smile spreads over her face. She moves in to take the seat beside him, crosses one leg over the other, and bares her knee. She leans slightly in the direction of Sleepy and looks directly at him with her inviting smile.

Sleepy

With his mouth still open to breathe, and exceptionally drowsy from the drugs, feels that his nostril is running. He gropes first in his trouser pockets and then in his breast pocket, never taking his eyes off the action on the screen. As usual Sleepy, has no handkerchief, but this doesn't worry him at all. He simply rubs his right index finger along the offending nostril and brushes it off on his jacket.

At this moment he remembers a bottle of nose spray in his pocket and takes it out with his right hand. Still deeply involved in the movie, he transfers the bottle to his left hand, unscrews the cap, and, eyes still on the screen,

balances the cap on his knee. Then, using the middle finger of his right hand, with pressure on the side, he stops his right nostril while he administers three little squirts of nose drops to his left nostril.

He then squirts the nose drops, after transferring the bottle to the other hand, into his right nostril. He tests each nostril with a couple of good sniffs.

Lady

This is too much for the refined tastes of our lady. She draws back from this display of vulgarity with an expression of disgust.

Sleepy

Attracted by this movement looks at the lady on his right side. He is holding the bottle in his right hand at a fixed point in front of his chest. He looks for several long moments at this woman who is, in turn, looking at him in disbelief. He looks at his bottle and back to the lady, wondering, ''Could she want my drops?'' and offers them to her.

Lady

This is too offensive. She moves to the vacant seat on her right, settles, and gives him a final look of absolute disgust.

Sleepy

Not understanding, but too tired to be overly concerned, puts the cap on the bottle and the bottle back in his right pocket. A couple of little sniffles and he looks back up at the screen, crossing his ankles and folding his arms. Reasonably comfortable, his mouth drops open as he watches the movie again.

Masher

Enters, removes his hat, comes down SR aisle, and selects an imaginary row of seats. Half-way along, he tries to sit but there is another customer occupying the seat. The customer starts up, making a threatening gesture. The Masher gropes along the row to the SL aisle.

Continuing down the aisle, and craning his neck, he notices the seat between Sleepy and Lady. He heads for it, disturbing Ma and Pa.

Sleepy, who has fallen asleep, has spread his knees. The Masher accidently puts his foot between them and for a moment their legs are all tangled up. They get straightened out, and Masher sits down.

Masher crosses his right leg over his left knee and plops his fedora on his right knee as a hat rack. He wets his fingers on his tongue and conceitedly slicks back an unruly lock of his hair.

Ma & Pa

Have resettled and are again involved in the film.

Sleepy

Gradually allows his head to fall on his chest and, quite content, sleeps.

Lady

Becomes aware of the good-looking man on her left and goes into action. Slowly she crosses her right leg over her left knee, allowing her foot to rub against the masher's ankle.

Masher

Not moving for a moment, inclines his head and slowly looks down at the lady's foot. Still uncommitted, he looks out over the audience and leans back with his upper body until he is behind the line of the lady's vision.

Only then does he slowly turn his head and eyes right in order to take a good look at the lady. A quick smile of pleasure crosses his face, as he finds her attractive.

With a slight, conceited swagger of his head, he slicks his hair once again, lifts his hat and recrosses his left leg over his right knee the better to resume the contact with the lady's foot. They lean shoulders together and remain in this position.

Sleepy

Who has been asleep, sits upright and, all of a sudden, falls to his left so that his head rests on Pa's shoulder.

Pa

Freezes in astonishment for a few seconds. Then, with his elbow, gives Sleepy a little shove, just enough for Sleepy to return to the vertical, totter for a brief instant, and fall to the other side.

Masher

Has decided to press his advantage and is about to put his right arm around the Lady's shoulders when Sleepy's head lands with a thump on his shoulder. The Masher gives Sleepy a bash on the head with the palm of his hand and continues to place his arm around the Lady.

Sleepy

Is startled by the Masher's blow. He flails his arms as if to defend himself. Finally realizing that he is still in the movie theatre, settles down and attempts to stay awake.

Masher

Tries to make himself comfortable with the Lady, but finds the broad rim of her hat awkward. He eventually holds it up off her cheek and they settle down.

Pa

Takes a cellophane bag of popcorn from his inside breast pocket. He makes a big fuss about tearing the top off the bag. He shakes it several times, obviously making a racket, devouring the popcorn and picking up crumbs.

Ma

Engrossed in the movie and reflecting the tearful story of the film in her own countenance, puts her hand out and holds Pa's hand to keep it from shaking the cellophane bag.

Sleepy

Has closed his eyes, asleep again.

Pa

Very carefully, and with his eyes on Ma, puts his cellophane bag, which is in his left hand, down by his right side. With his right hand, he quietly takes a piece of popcorn and starts to put it to his mouth, hoping Ma won't notice.

Sleepy

Once again drops his head onto Pa's right shoulder.

Pa

Stops for a brief instant, decides that there is no harm done and continues to eat his popcorn.

Ma

Beautifully involved, Ma looks at Pa with tear-filled eyes and a sad little smile on her lips. When she notices Sleepy snuggling into Pa's shoulder, she looks front, and the smile fades. Ma stands to exit, pulling Pa behind her. When she reaches the aisle, she lets Pa pass and then re-enters the row and takes Pa's seat, expecting him to take hers. She gives Sleepy a dirty look.

Sleepy

When Pa moves his supporting shoulder away, Sleepy almost falls but is awake enough to regain an upright position and breathe a big sigh.

Pa

In the meantime has wandered to the exit doors and looks around for Ma. He returns and finds her still seated. He accepts this and sits, quietly finishing his popcorn and settles to watch the rest of the film.

Sleepy

Tries valiantly to keep his eyes open: they keep closing, he comes to with a start. Sleepy makes a decided effort and, holding his eyes open, slowly bends forward. Literally asleep with his eyes open. Comatose, his eyes roll, and still he bends further forward until, finally, he saves himself from landing on the floor with one hand. He sits half asleep again but vertical for a moment, then falls abruptly on Ma's shoulder.

Ma

For a moment is about to object.

Sleepy

Sensing a feminine shoulder, is reminded of his childhood and snuggles, content at last.

Pa

Has finished his popcorn some time ago and is now more into the film. A particularly funny bit strikes him, and he elbows Ma in the ribs. The blow caroms right through Ma and strikes Sleepy who bounces up to the vertical again. His head makes a little circular motion as he struggles to regain his balance before he again falls toward the Masher.

Masher

Just about to embrace the Lady, stops when he feels Sleepy's head to consider how to deal with it.

Lady

Very gently puts her finger on Sleepy's forehead and softly pushes him back to the vertical, holding him there for a moment, before she removes her finger. She smiles at the Masher and they are just about to kiss as the theme music comes up to mark the end of the film. The Lady and the Masher rise and go up the right aisle, arms around each other.

Ma & Pa

Ma, who has been twisting Pa's hat out of shape, is quite openly weeping. Pa retrieves his rumpled hat as they slowly exit up the left aisle.

Sleepy

Remains seated, fast asleep with his head still in the awkward position the Lady had left it.

Ma

Notices the nice young man is still asleep and quickly comes back down the aisle to shake him.

Sleepy

Comes to with a start and, quite confused, applauds. He realizes where he is and quickly exits with the rest as the lights fade to black.

An epic poem by Charles Max Cohen adapted by Adrian Pecknold as a poemime *Land Before Time*.

Erotic Art Observed

Précis

A display of imaginary statues sculptured in very erotic poses are being shown in the local art gallery.

Into this scene wanders a very naive rural type in tune with all natural biological functions, a very prim, straight-laced woman conditioned to believe implicitly in fire and brimstone, a well-meaning fairly liberal minister of the faith who believes that he has an image to uphold, and a constable of law and order who has somewhat the same beliefs.

The sketch explores their individual reactions to the shocking pieces of sculpture, their actions when fully comprehending the show and their relationships as each enters and exits.

Mimedrama

Players	A Farmer
	Miss Prim
	The Minister
	The Constable
Properties	Three L-shaped Bauhaus boxes are placed SL, DSC and SR. They are the bases for three imaginary pieces of very erotic sculpture.

Farmer

Enters from USL. He is a little uncertain and hastily removes his straw hat when he realizes he is in the gallery. He slowly goes to the piece SL and examines it closely, not quite sure what it is intended to represent. Finally he recognizes the intention and he points and almost lets out a guffaw and looks around for someone with whom to share his appreciation.

He stifles his laughter and slowly continues to move across to the piece SR, but refers back once or twice to the piece SL, with a broad grin. He stops and gives his attention to the new piece. Immediately he understands its intent and he can't resist miming the milking of a cow, taking great delight in this comparison with what he sees in the statue.

Warming to his inspection he moves to the piece CS. This is a little more puzzling. He turns his head on its left side. Still puzzled he turns his head on its right side. A slow broad grin breaks on his face. He points his finger dead centre on the imaginary statue and tickles some protrusion. He slaps his side with his hat at the humour in this piece of erotic whimsy and he almost doubles up as he starts to exit.

Miss Prim

Enters from USL almost colliding with the Farmer as he exits USR, stifling his laughter. Quite amazed at this open display of emotion, she very disapprovingly looks after him and then gives her attention to the statue on the SL base. She bends slightly forward for a closer look.

With an absolutely neutral expression she straightens up. She backs up slowly across the stage not taking her eyes off the sculpture. When she reaches SR she stops and gives a little shudder, which she controls, and we are not sure whether it is vicarious delight or censoring disapproval.

She turns and examines the new piece. Now she begins to shake slightly. She opens her mouth and gulps air. She is very disturbed and goes to the DS piece. Here, she turns her head slightly left, then right. Now she compresses her hands to her groin almost as if needing the bathroom. A little smile of pleasure crosses her face. She is flustered and flushed. She pats her face. She gulps more air.

Quickly she goes to USC. She looks off to the left and sees someone coming. In a dither she steps this way, then that and hastily exits USR.

Minister

A beat later enters from USL and crosses almost to USR in a beckoning posture, as if he had hoped to stop Miss Prim and have a little chat. He is wearing a preacher's collar and a bowler hat. He removes his hat, disappointed that he missed meeting Miss Prim, he turns to examine the sculpture SL.

He holds his hat with both hands on the brim, in front of his chest. He puts on a smile of beatitude, in anticipation of his delight in all things artistic. He examines the piece still wearing an anticipatory smile. He goes a step up and a little behind the statue. He freezes.

Very slowly, the smile fades to a neutral, then almost disapproving look of righteousness as he backs away and turns to the piece SR. The moment he sees this piece he gives a little start and puts his hand to his mouth in disbelief.

He turns to the DSC piece. Similar to the others he puts his head to the left, then to the right, almost standing on his head to decipher this very erotic piece. With sudden comprehension, he straightens up quickly, not knowing quite what to do. He attempts to cover the offending centre with his hat, but realizes this would not be the best hat rack. He

becomes aware of his compromising position and begins to exit. He sees someone coming and flattens himself against the wall hoping that he will not be seen.

Constable

Enters from USL. He is looking very stern. He goes to the left statue, takes a notebook and pencil from his pocket and jots down a reference. He continues to the DS piece and turns the page.

Minister

At first wanting to flee, but seeing that the constable is doing his duty, he slowly approaches him from behind, nodding his approval. He looks over his shoulder to see what notes the constable is recording.

Constable

It becomes apparent that the Constable, far from taking notes, is actually making a drawing of the statue, and enjoying it.

Minister

When he finally sees what the Constable is drawing, he loses his look of righteousness and steps down to give the Constable a terrible accusing look.

Constable

Putting his pencil and notebook away, gestures, "Who, me?"

Minister

Accusingly nods his head, "Yes."

Constable

Shakes his head, "no," and with his US forefinger accusingly taps the Minister on his chest, "You."

Minister

Comprehending that the tables are turned pleads, "Oh, no!"

Constable

Takes the Minister by the back of his jacket and leads him offstage, USR to a blackout.

Ensemble

The Electrocution

Précis

The soon to be widowed wife, the prison padre and the executioner attend at midnight the final ritualistic ceremony of the condemned. When the electrical equipment fails to work the first three, for individual and personal reasons, impatiently try to correct the malfunctioning fuse box. As a result of their impatience and haste, the condemned husband gets a ring-side seat from the electric chair as the tables are turned.

Mimedrama

Players	The Executioner
	The Minister
	The Prisoner's Wife
	The Husband

Properties	An arm chair, or grouping
	of L Boxes at centre stage
	A hangman's hood

(Sound effects of an electrical buzzing, and the twelve o'clock striking of a distant clock.)

Executioner
Sits in the arm chair, CS. He is eating his snack, a sandwich and meticulously picking up and eating any stray crumb which happens to fall on his serviette. After a few moments we hear the distant sounding of the clock. He holds still and listens for a moment.

He hastily gobbles the last bite of his sandwich, picks up a few stray crumbs and shakes out his serviette. He stands and pulls the serviette over his head. We now see it is the hood with two eyeholes.

He now goes through a very militaristic testing of his equipment. He tests imaginary arm clamp on the SL arm of the chair. He tests the imaginary head clamp above the back of the chair. He tests in succession the SR arm of the chair, the SR leg and the SL leg. He stands to attention.

He marches DS, does left turn and marches two or three paces to DSL. He opens an imaginary fuse box and manipulates one or two fuses. He closes the box and pulls the master switch down. *(There is the sound of buzzing and a perceptible dimming of the lights.)* He pushes the master switch back. *(The lights come back up to full and the sound stops.)* He repeats this one more time, then does an about turn and stands at ease. He folds his arms, apparently ready to do his job at the right time.

Minister
Enters from USR in a very stylized slow march. His hands are in a prayerful attitude, his head bowed. He wears a traditional preacher's collar. He proceeds a few paces onstage, does a right turn and comes DS. He does a left turn and slow marches over to the Executioner. He stops just short and turns back on stage.

Wife
Timed to be about three or four paces behind the Minister, the Wife enters dressed already in black and sniffing at a black lace kerchief. She turns a little US at the same time as the Minister.

Husband
Enters similarly, but with less ritual, a little out of step, and comes down, intrigued with the awesomeness of the electric chair. He stops in front of the Minister.

Minister
Forcefully indicates that the condemned kneel. He gives a blessing and does the Sign of the Cross over the husband. *(Husband crosses himself.)*

Wife
Puts the back of her hand to her forehead in an obviously melodramatic and phony display of grief.

Minister
Indicates to the Husband, "Rise."

Husband
Rises and turns to face front.

Minister
Indicates to the Husband, "Sit."

Husband
Remains standing, gesturing imploringly, as his lips do a silent stuttering, "bbbbbbu."

Minister

Indifferently gives the back of his hand to the Husband's chest, "Oh, do sit."

Husband

Sits as a result of the push and looks to his wife.

Wife

Looks away from this pitiable sight, dabbing the phony tears from her eyes.

Minister

Signals to the Executioner.

Executioner

Goes into action. He goes to the left arm of the condemned and fastens the imaginary clamp, pinning his wrist to the chair. He fastens the head clamp around the forehead.

Husband

This effectively pinions the prisoner's head so that now, only his eyes can follow the action around him.

Executioner

Fastens the right arm, but before he can shut the clamp, the prisoner removes his arm. The Executioner stares steadily at the Husband.

Husband

Slowly returns his arm to the clamp.

Executioner

Continues. He finishes the right arm, clamps the right leg, then the left. He gives a comforting pat to the Husband's head and returns to fold his arms in readiness at the fuse box.

Minister

Crosses to the Wife. He takes her hand and caresses it in comfort.

Wife

Who has been in an attitude of head up, as though looking for divine intervention, gives a little coquettish smile of pleasure. She immediately disguises this in the proper attitude of appropriate grief and places her head on the Minister's chest.

Minister

Puts his arm around the Wife and pats her shoulder. The embrace becomes tentatively involving as they look into each others eyes.

Husband

Bravely holds back his tears as he witnesses this display of compassion out of the extreme right corners of his eyes.

Executioner

A little impatient, snaps to attention.

Minister

Startled slightly by this, gives a downward signal with his arm for the Executioner to proceed. Then he takes the Wife in a comforting embrace, trying not to look at these last horrible moments.

Executioner

Does an about face. He reaches and pulls the master handle down. *(There is nothing.)*

Husband

Is rapidly turning his eyes from the Executioner SL, to his Wife and the Minister, SR, and back again and again.

Wife

Looks around the Minister to the Executioner and does a "What's the matter?" gesture.

Minister

Shakes his hand, "Quickly, try again."

Executioner

Slowly and determinedly tries again. Still nothing. He opens the fuse box and starts to undo fuses.

Wife

Dashes over and is about to push the Executioner out of the way, convinced that she will be able to make it work.

Minister

Follows her and they are all poking around in the fuse box. *(Suddenly sound effects of buzzing and the lights dim.)*

The Executioner, the Wife and the Minister stiffen and shake for a moment as the power effects them. They slide to the floor in a heap.

Husband

Has been watching this last out of the corner of his eye. When the pile of bodies is settled he looks to the audience. Then with his fastened hands he gestures in a palms up and out attitude of "C'est la vie," and the lights go to black.

The Rape

Précis

The paradox of involvement or apathy and rewards or punishment, posed without answer.

A man and a woman await a bus. Two toughs rob and attempt to rape the woman. In the first telling, the man flees the scene early and presumably lives.

The identical tale is retold with the man attempting to save the woman; the woman escapes and the man is killed.

Mimedrama

Players	A Man, No. 1, reserved, cold, self-centred; No. 2, open, warm, outgoing
	A Woman, aware, responsible
	Hood No. 1, cruel, neurotic, impatient
	Hood No. 2, A follower, easily swayed

First Scenario

Man

Enters from DSR and crosses left, looking off for bus. It is not coming so he backs US a pace or two and prepares to wait.

Woman

Enters in rush from DSR crossing left and satisfied she is in time, eases back to CS rummaging in her real purse to find imaginary compact which she uses quickly and efficiently to repair her makeup after a rushed, busy day, and settles to wait, glancing openly at the man.

Man

Who has been watching her actions. He looks away guiltily, not wanting to relate.

Woman

Turns back, prepared to wait for the bus.

Hood No. 1

Enters from USL, shadow-boxing and in general, role-playing a real tough guy.

Hood No. 2

Follows immediately, encouraging and hero-worshipping Hood No. 1.

Hood No 1

Notices Woman, gives indicative nod and lustful signal to Hood No. 2 and comes down slightly to her right.

Hood No. 2

Comes down a little to her left and behind her.

Woman

Sees Hood No. 1 and tenses.

Hood No. 1

Suddenly grabs the purse and backs off R, teasing the girl to "Come and get it."

Woman

Makes a dash and grabs for the purse.

Hood No. 1

Throws it to Hood No. 2, L of C.

Woman

Immediately runs to Hood No. 2 attempting to retrieve her purse.

Hood No. 2

Circles US and throws the purse to Hood No. 1, and continues around to join him, SR.

Woman

Is at CS, helpless and reaching futilely after her purse. She turns with a quick beseeching gesture to the Man at SL.

Man

Quickly turns his back to her, ignoring her plea.

Woman

Again turns towards Hoods.

Hood No. 1

Opens the purse and starts to rifle through it.

Woman

Makes an angry dash to stop him.

Hood No. 2

Grabs her as she passes and forcefully swings her US and around at the same time putting a Half-Nelson wrestling hold around her neck with her left arm, holding her, with his other hand spread suggestively over her left breast. He leers lustfully, looking to No. 1 for approval.

Hood No. 1

Waits while this was happening, then continues to rifle through the purse. He tosses a few imaginary things offstage R, then upturns the purse shaking it out, and finding it empty, suddenly stops cold and stares threateningly at the Woman.

Woman

Senses the sexual threat in his look and opens her mouth to scream.

Hood No. 2

With lascivious drooling smile, clamps his right hand quickly over her mouth, stopping her scream.

Hood No. 1

Violently throws purse to a position USC. (A dramatic change to blue flood and slow-motion actions, or alternatively, strobe lights.) He reaches for the woman's feet and ankles and lifts them up, spreading her legs and forcing his body between them.

Woman

Simulates resistance, kicking her legs in slow motion as they carry her USC to where the purse was thrown.

Hood No. 2

When in position US, technically goes to the floor backwards, taking the girl with him and Hood No. 1 following up his advantage to a simulated rape.

Man

In slow motion, and frightened to death that he will become involved, runs straight across the DS area and off, SR.

(Lights to blackout, during which the Woman recovers purse and rolls off SR and Hoods roll off SL. General lights up.)

Second Scenario
Man

Enters from DSR and crosses L, looking off for bus. It is not coming so he backs US a pace or two and prepares to wait.

Woman

Enters in a rush from DSR, crossing L, and satisfied

that she is in time eases back to SC, rummaging in her purse for her compact. She fixes her make-up, then prepares to wait, glancing openly at the man.

Man

Returns her smile with a slight nod of fellow-traveller understanding.

Hood No. 1

Enters from USL, shadow-boxing.

Hood No. 2

Immediately follows in hero-worship.

Hood No. 1

Notices Woman, gives indicative nod and lustful signal to Hood No. 2, and slowly comes down on her right.

Hood No. 2

Comes down a little to her left and behind her.

Man

Sensing a threatening atmosphere, takes a quick step more onstage, the better to see what Hood No. 1 is doing.

Woman

Sees Hood No. 1 and tenses.

Hood No. 1

Suddenly grabs purse and backs off R, teasing the Woman to "Come and get it."

Woman

Makes a dash and grabs for the purse.

Hood No. 1

Throws the purse to Hood No. 2, L of C.

Woman

Immediately runs to Hood No. 2.

Hood No. 2

Circles upstage and throws the purse to Hood No. 1, and continues around to join him, SR.

Woman

Is left helpless at CS, reaching futilely after her purse.

Man

Steps quickly to her side as if to protect her.

Hood No. 2

Pulls an imaginary switchblade and steps down between them and Hood No. 1.

Hood No. 1

Opens purse and starts to rifle through it.

Woman

Makes an angry dash to stop him.

Hood No. 2

Grabs her as she passes and forcefully swings her US and around at the same time putting a Half-Nelson wrestling hold around her neck with his left arm, and holding the switchblade with his other hand, the point against her throat.

Man

Makes a start to intercede but has to stop as he sees the danger to the Woman.

Hood No. 1

Waits a beat while this is happening, then continues to rifle through purse. He tosses some imaginary things offstage R, shakes out the empty purse, then suddenly stops and stares threateningly at the Woman.

Woman

Senses the sexual threat in his look and opens her mouth to scream.

Hood No. 2

Not wanting to cut her throat at this point, has to release the Half-Nelson and bring his left hand over her face to stop the scream.

Hood No. 1

Violently throws the purse USC,

(Lights: dramatic change, as before)

In slow motion, he continues and reaches for the Woman's feet and lifts them up, spreading her legs and forcing his body between them.

Man

Intervenes as they are carrying the Woman US. He grabs Hood No. 1 around the head and pulls him back and DSL.

Hood No. 2

Releases the girl and goes for the Man, with switchblade held high, still in his right hand.

Woman

Finds her purse and exits USL.

Hood No. 1.

Rolls his head out of Man's grasp and grabs his left

arm swinging him (slow motion) US, and around and down to CS.

Hood No. 2

With his left hand grabs the Man's right arm and between him and Hood No. 1, they spread-eagle the man backwards as Hood No. 2, still in slow motion, brings the switchblade relentlessly towards the Man's exposed belly and plunges it in.

Man

Continues his propulsion, but draws his arms in to hold the spouting wound and continues to the floor.

Hoods No. 1 and 2

Having released the Man's arms, watch as he slowly accepts the floor.

(Lights: Abrupt change to generals.)

Hood No. 1

Dashes USL and looks off, sees the Woman and follows.

Hood No. 2

Kicks man over, bends and pulls switchblade out of stomach, wiping it on Man's cloths. He kicks him savagely and follows Hood No. 1, emulating the original shadow-boxing.

Man

Makes a feeble attempt to rise but passes out as lights fade to black.

The Pub

Précis

A drunk has just been interdicted by the bartender who refuses him drink. Under duress he decides to leave. The task of putting on his trench coat (real) becomes more and more confusing. As other customers arrive we begin to see the environment through the eyes of the inebriate. People do weird things, bars disassemble and reassemble. In the end the drunk is thoroughly confused.

Mimedrama

Players	Drunk
	Three patrons
Properties	Trench coat
	Seat or L Box

Drunk

Is discovered, sitting on his trench coat on a box, SL at an imaginary table. He is a little wobbly and rubbery in the neck. He ripples his lips with the fingers of his right hand as you sometimes see very thirsty people do with an uncontrolled gesture.

He very carefully reaches out, takes an imaginary glass off the table and brings it to his lips. By the way he drinks it is obviously empty. He turns it upside down and shakes it, as though this will produce some more drink. He runs his finger around the inside and then licks it.

Noticing that the imaginary bartender, DSR, is looking at him he holds the glass wobbly on high in a gesture of "another drink." The bartender obviously says something disrespectful, by the drunks reaction. Slowly and carefully, he replaces the glass on the table. He then stands, wobbly, and gives a "The same to you" gesture to the bartender.

He takes his trench coat by the collar and puts his left arm in the right arm of the coat. He makes another rude gesture to the bartender and puts his arm and coat behind him and slides his right arm back and down into the left arm of the coat and then attempts to pull it up over his shoulders. It bulges awkwardly inside out at his neck.

He turns around himself like a puppy chasing the tail of his coat. He turns back, DS, taking his left arm out of the coat. He takes the right sleeve of the coat by the cuff and tries to peer up it to find the trouble.

He bunches it up, as a stocking might be prepared, and puts his hand successfully through it. He wiggles his fingers and, as if this was the problem, looks a wobbly but superior look at the bartender.

Customer 1

Enters through imaginary swing doors, USC. He comes down and as he passes the drunk he stops, then walks backwards left, right, left and then forward again, as if it was the most natural thing in the world.

Drunk

As the customer is coming down, he holds out his hand in a begging attitude. As No. 1 walks backward, the drunk begins to turn away for the three paces and then turns back as the customer re-passes him.

Customer No.1

Continues to DSR and takes an attitude at the bar. He orders a drink and drinks it.

Drunk

Shakes his head as if to clear his senses and staggers back a pace.

Customer No. 2   *(Preferably a girl)*

Enters with a very exaggerated, sensuous walk and does exactly the same ritual as No. 1.

Drunk

Still asking for a hand out, this time staggers back to his seat, after the backwards walk.

Customer No. 2

Continues to the left of No. 1 and orders a drink.

Customer No. 1

Picks up his drink and moves behind, to the left of No. 2, in an obvious pick-up attempt.

Drunk

Gets unsteadily to his feet and is about to join this little gathering, hand out, asking for a drink.

Customer No. 3

Enters and the same ritual occurs. He then continues to the bar, to the left of No. 1. This puts him almost DSC. He orders his drink, takes a sip. All three are now standing in a row across, DSR. Their arms are resting with forearms on the bar, touching elbow to elbow.

Drunk

Unsteadily, draws down a little, and about a pace to the left of No. 3.

Ordering Routine

No. 2 looking R raises her left hand in an ordering gesture, followed by No. 1, and then No. 3. In a delayed broken rhythm the drunk raises his left hand tentatively with a lick of his lips. He stands slightly rubbery, waiting.

The routine continues and No. 2. drinks and returns to rested forearms. This is followed by No. 1, and No. 3. As No. 3. rests his arms on the bar, the drunk reaches out towards the end of the bar.

Just out of reach the bar appears to slant down. *(Elbow to elbow and maintaining a straight line.)* No. 3. leans a little from the waist, sideways, lowering his left arm and raising his right arm. No. 1 and No. 2 adjust at the same time to create the illusion that the bar is slanting up into SR.

The drunk strains to reach the bar with his right arm and they all hold this counter slant for a beat. The vertical line of the drunk's body is slanted as grossly to SL as the mime can accomplish and yet maintain control. It slowly realigns as does the drunk with a slight silent hiccup which he politely covers with his right hand.

The drunk now looks at this end of the bar. He shakes his head and elongates his neck for a closer look. The arms of the three customers ripple as a wave down the row to the SR end. The drunk shakes his head and looks away a moment to clear his senses. He looks back and the bar ripples back from R to L and reels the drunk back up with his eyes almost coma-like, and he knocks his head to clear.

The ordering routine is repeated and ends once again with the drunk out of rhythm, still hopefully ordering. The drinks are served and this time No. 2 takes her drink and crosses US of the rest, over to SL. As she crosses the drunk he reaches out and takes the drink out of her right hand with his left hand. He quickly drinks the drink and hands the glass back, very smug but still unsteady.

She accepts the glass back with her left hand. At the same time she swings her right hand down and back and gives the drunk a slap on his DS cheek *(sound effects and electronic boing-boing music)* which sends the drunk into a slow spin to the floor.

During this, the bar disassembles and reforms SL. The drunk crawls along the floor to SR of the bar. He rises and tries to grab the right end. The bar continues to circle much as a "crack the whip" with the three members using the heel-toe shuffle to move in a concentric circle. This draws the drunk to his chair and the coat. At this point, the bar SOBERS and the members walk naturally, but determinedly, off stage.

The drunk continues to reach for the elusive end of the bar. He grabs his coat and now follows the customers up, but arriving USC he splats against the US wall and oozes to the floor as the lights fade.

The First Mirror

Précis

Based on an Oriental legend.

Scene 1
Working in his garden, a Japanese gardener unearths a mirror and, never having seen such an object and not understanding physics, thinks that he has uncovered a reincarnated form of his honourable ancestor.

Scene 2
He hides the mirror in his house. Overcome with curiosity, his wife takes the object while he is sleeping and, seeing her reflection, thinks that her husband is having an affair with a special geisha girl.

Her husband decides they will take the object to a wise person who lives at some distance. They start their journey.

Scene 3
They are accosted by a bandit. The husband offers the mirror and the bandit, seeing the reflection of such a ferocious warrior, flees in terror.

Scene 4
The couple come to a river where a boatman demands payment to ferry them across. On being offered the mirror, the boatman doubles up with laughter at his comical reflection. He is delighted at this amusement and he takes them across.

Scene 5
The wise person at the temple explains the mirror to them and happily they rush home.

Scene 6
At home they take turns playing with the mirror until the wife accidently drops it and it breaks. They are downcast until the husband, realizing that it was only a piece of glass forgives his wife and they embrace.

Mimedrama

Players	Young man
	Wife
	Bandit
	Boatman
	Wise Elder

Properties	Scene 1:	A field. Gnarled bush or stump cut-out USL.
	Scene 2:	Home. Open door piece, framed with opaque paper with oriental design USC. Oriental bed throw, floor SL.
	Scene 3:	The Forest. Gnarled bush USR. Higher gnarled tree USL.
	Scene 4:	A River. Gnarled tree USC, gnarled bush USR.
	Scene 5:	A Temple. Oriental entrance cut-out USC. Low devotional altar DSR.
	Scene 6:	Home. As in Scene 2.

The scenes are bridged with simple flute (or similar) music starting before the scene end to cover the set change in blackout and continuing into next scene, then fading out.

Scene 1

(Music fades out after lights up.)

Young Man
Enters at a little jog run from SR with an imaginary hoe over his shoulder. He stops at the stump and leans the hoe against the stump.

He feels the heat from the imaginary sun and takes off his shirt and folds it over the stump.

He takes up the hoe and runs to a point DSR where he hoes the first furrow with chopping movements, across to DSL; he places the hoe against the stump and, as he jogs back to the start of the row, he reaches into an imaginary pocket for a handful of seeds.

He proceeds to drop the seeds a bit apart into the furrow, each time tapping the earth with his bare foot. He stops once to react to the sun and mop his brow with his forearm. He completes the row, returns the unused seeds to his pocket, retrieves his hoe, jogs back to SR and repeats a second row SR to SL. Leaning his hoe against the stump, he takes seeds from his pocket and proceeds as before. Half-way through the row, his aim is bad and he misses the furrow. He stoops, retrieves the seed and correctly places it, tapping it and reacting again to the heat of the sun. He continues to the end of the row.

He brushes the dust off his hands, retrieves his hoe from the stump and jogs to SR to start row three. Half-way into the row, his hoe meets some resistance. He pulls, strains slightly and loosens the object a little.

He throws his hoe out of his way, kneels and uses his hands to free the soil around what appears to be a flat circular object, a third of a metre in diameter. He brushes most of the dirt off it.

He examines it closely. Thinking he sees something bright, he briskly rubs it with his forearm and again peers into it. Never having seen his reflection, his eyes slowly widen, his mouth opens and slackens, as he comes to the awesome realization that he has unearthed a portrait of his honourable ancestor. In fear and trepidation he drops the mirror, face down, and scurries behind the stump, cowering. Gradually he realizes the ancestor is not going to wreak vengeance on him. Slowly he crawls back to the mirror, tentatively reaches out his arm and gingerly lifts one edge of the mirror. He loses courage, drops the mirror and cowers again. Once again he gains confidence, slowly he lifts the mirror, and looks — at his honourable ancestor! He quickly bows his head three times, in obeisance.

He looks uncertainly to left and right. What should he do? He slowly stands, looking around. Should he hide it?

An idea lights up his face; he will take it home and hide it. Resolved now, he gently places the mirror on the ground, bows quickly three times, jogs to the stump for his shirt, starts putting it on and jogs back to the mirror. He picks up the mirror in both hands, bows quickly again three times, carefully places the mirror next to his body under his shirt and does his shirt up, securing the mirror with his arm. He looks left to make sure he hasn't been observed and jogs off SR.

(The music comes up as the lights fade to blackout.)

Scene 2

(Set change in blackout. Lights up — music fades.)

Wife

Discovered plumping an imaginary pillow on a bed SL. She gracefully rises from her knees and, with her hands softly folded in her kimono sleeves, walks quickly in small steps to an imaginary linen closet DSR.

She slides open the door from L to R and reaches up to the top shelf to take out an imaginary folded bedspread. She places it over her left arm and closes the door. As she returns to the bed, she opens the spread, preparing to lay it on the bed. She half-kneels to straighten the on-stage side, then stops abruptly and listens. She quickly rises and runs to US and slides open the imaginary door. She steps out and looks off expectantly SR. No one is there. She comes back inside, closes the door and goes to the off-stage side of the bed. She reaches up and pulls an imaginary lamp down to her height. She steadies the lamp with one hand and slowly turns the wick up with the other.

(Lights fade up brighter.)

Wife

Raises the lamp to its original position and kneels to straighten the spread. She looks up at the door, quickly runs and opens it, leans out looking SR and then turns and stands obediently, head and eyes downcast, hands folded, waiting.

Young Man
Jogs from SR to US of the door. With the toe of one foot, he flicks the slipper from the other and repeats, bending to straighten them neatly at SR of door. He enters and bows slowly, acknowledging his wife.

Wife
Smilingly returns the bow, closes the door behind him and stands waiting, again.

Young Man
Holding the hidden mirror protectively under his arm, he looks around the room. His head and eyes rest briefly as he spies the imaginary linen closet. He looks furtively sideways at his wife and then jogs to the closet. He opens the door and reaches inside his shirt for the mirror. He stops and casts a quick look US at his wife.

Wife
Who has been straining to see her husband's unusual behaviour quickly lowers her head to her previous attitude of obeisance before he can catch her watching him.

Young Man
Satisfied that she is not looking, he lifts one or two layers of linen and slips the mirror in between them. He looks quickly back to his wife.

Wife
Incredulous and curious, once again adopts previous attitude.

Young Man
Satisfied and pleased that he has temporarily solved his dilemma, he adopts a prayerful attitude with his hands, bows reverently three times and quickly closes the linen closet door. He turns and starts for the bed, shedding his shirt.

Wife
Anticipating this, she comes quickly DS, turns the on-stage side of the bedspread back and proceeds down and around the offstage side to wait.

Young Man
Neatly folds his shirt and places it US of his imaginary pillow. He lies down facing onstage and pulls the imaginary spread over his legs.

Wife
Bows once, reaches up for the lamp, pulls it down, steadies it with both hands and then, with one hand, turns it down. (*Lights fade abruptly to low key.*)

Wife
Takes off her kimono and places it at the head of the bed. She kneels and pulls down the spread, slips under it, and, lying on her back, pulls it up. Three beats go by. Her curiosity gets the better of her and, slowly, she raises her head and shoulders, resting on her arms. She looks at her husband and then at the linen closet.

Young Man
On physical touch cue from wife, turns from his side to his back.

Wife
Quickly lies back. Three beats go by. Slowly she repeats resting on her arms. Once again she looks at her husband and then to the linen closet. Persisting, she reaches to throw off the spread but . . .

Young Man
Continues to turn to his left side, throwing his right arm across his wife.

Wife
Freezes, obviously alarmed; three beats go by. She looks again to the closet, then to her husband. Very slowly and gingerly she takes his right wrist with her right finger and thumb and gently places his arm along his hip. She stealthily eases back the spread and gets out of bed. She tip-toes around the top of the bed, watching him every moment. She stops, looks at the closet, then back to her husband: satisfied that she has not awakened him, she quickly crosses to the closet.

Young Man
Hearing her, quickly sits up, looking in the direction of the closet. With his left arm he makes a cautionary gesture toward the space

where he imagines his wife to be sleeping. He slowly rises and as he does so, picks up the kimono and prepares it as a net, stealthily approaching the figure he sees dimly at the closet.

Wife
Having arrived at the closet, very slowly slides the door open, and on tip-toe feels between the folded linen with her right hand. When she discovers something, she reaches up with her other hand and withdraws the mirror with both hands.
(The lights have very slowly crept up.)

Young Man
At this very moment, throws the kimono over her head and pulls her back and completely around and past himself, ending up somewhat SC with his wife on his right. He pulls the kimono off her head.

With an even count of one, two, three, he looks aghast at his wife, turns his head and looks incredulously at his wife's vacant place in bed, and turns back to his wife with a helpless, hopeless attitude, allowing the kimono to drop slowly to the floor.

Wife
A little dazed by all this, and puzzled at the actions of her lunatic husband, slowly looks into the mirror.

Seeing her reflection, she is at first startled, but then, believing that her husband has brought the portrait of another woman into the house, looks tearfully at him. Terribly hurt, she looks again into the mirror. New anger rises within her. She sticks her tongue out at the portrait, and is immediately startled and aghast that this impertinent and mysterious female has the audacity to stick her tongue out at an honourable obedient wife. Not realizing the absurdity of her thoughts, she thrusts the mirror into her husband's hands and moves right a pace, turning her back on him petulant and hurt.

Young Man
Watching this incredible behaviour, he looks into the mirror, makes three quick little ritualistic bows, and looks back to his wife.

Wife
Snaps her glance back to her husband, then, in a quick change of attitude, she puts her nose haughtily in the air. Her mouth breaks into a syrupy sweet smile and she does a grotesque parody of a geisha girl. She undulates to SR, miming the combing of her imaginary long hair, turning and sensuously approaching her husband, gracefully strumming an imaginary stringed instrument. She allows the instrument to fade away and, with a continuing motion of her left hand, softly strokes his right cheek, drawing him around on his spot as she circles around him, up and back to his right side.

She stops, and with her right hand strokes his left cheek and ends with a small but sharp slap to his cheek and petulantly half turns her back to him.

Young Man
Who had been witnessing this display in absolute puzzlement, drawing his head back as she stroked him, now feels his cheek with his left hand.

He shakes his head in exasperation, taking a breath. Then, suddenly, he stops: he gets an idea.

Standing where he is, he looks up and offstage right, quickly back to mirror, bows, and then looks at his wife.

He nods his head, quick and decisive. He bends, picks up the kimono and thrusts it into his wife's hands. He goes to the head of the bed, places the mirror flat upon it and wraps it in his shirt.

Wife
Having put her kimono on and seeing her husband's actions, anticipates him and goes to the door, opens it and awaits him there. *(Music)*

Young Man
Places the shirt package under his arm, steps through the door and slips into his slippers.

Wife
Steps through door and closes it, slips her slippers on and follows her husband as they exit SR.

(The lights dim to black.)

Scene 3

(Lights up)

Bandit

Discovered centre stage in the pose of a Japanese warrior (Samurai) ready to defend himself, feet apart, knees bent and holding an imaginary sword, which is sheathed through an obi-like sash on his left side. His left hand is holding the top of imaginary scabbard, his head is down.

Slowly he raises his head, revealing a grotesque and ferocious grimace: he holds it a moment.

His face relaxes as he ponders. He gives a slight nod of satisfaction, shifts slightly, then lowers his head as if to start again. This time, he snaps his head up revealing an even more ferocious grimace, draws his sword and lunges straight at the audience. He holds the pose a moment, then breaks, as an actor coming out of a role, and struts as he sheathes his sword, head high, very satisfied.

He looks at stump SL; he will treat it as imaginary adversary. He strikes his warrior pose facing the stump, draws his sword and slashes: one; two; decapitating the innocent stump.

Whirling around, he is about to face the tree USR as a second foe. He raises his sword overhead in both hands and is about to slash. He freezes.

Quickly, he looks offstage L behind him and, in sudden fright, dashes to hide behind the tree, trembling and peeking out to SL.

The Canadian Mime Theatre production of the mimo-drama, *First Mirror*. L to R; Harro Masko, Ian Mackay, Robin Patterson.

Young Man

Showing signs of fatigue, jogs in from SL to C. He stops, looks offstage L and waits.

Wife

In her tiny steps, wearily arrives at her husband's side.

Young Man

Pats her consolingly on the shoulder and turns; they must proceed on their journey.

Bandit

On seeing that they are just two ordinary peasants, regains his courage. As they prepare to leave, he jumps out to block their path, striking his most ferocious pose, sword drawn over his head.

Young Man & Wife

Cower together.

Bandit

Approaches in three, slow, suspenseful steps. On the third step, he brings the sword slashing straight down, between them.

Young Man

Lets go of his wife, dashes behind the tree USR and cowers.

Wife

Dashes to behind the remains of the stump USL and crouches on her knees, out of sight.

Bandit

Recovers from his lunge and stalks the husband threateningly. He flushes the husband out to DSR by feigning an US assault, and then, mercilessly, closes in for the kill.

Young Man

Trembling in fear, fumbles in his shirt. As the bandit is about to slash him, the Young Man thrusts the mirror at him, under his nose, as a peace offering.

Bandit

Glimpsing the most ferocious bandit he has ever seen, leaps in fright and dashes USL behind the stump.

Wife

The Bandit propels the Wife, in a side roll, from her hiding place and she scurries on her hands and knees to behind the tree USR.

Young Man

Who has taken a few steps to USC, continues to hold the mirror high at his left arm's length. Now, he begins to tremble and his knees shake as he remembers the danger.

Bandit

Caught between two emotions; ventures from behind the stump. On the one hand he grimaces his most ferocious grimace, and on the other, he is terrified of the frightening personage hidden within this strange object.

As he slowly approaches, one arm holding his sword, he extends the other towards the husband's wrist in order to lower the object, that he might see it better. As he looks, his worst fears are confirmed. He leaps in fright and with long, quick strides, dashes off SL.

Young Man

Follows, looking off into space in puzzlement, moving DS a little. His ancient ancestor has protected him!

He bows three times and carefully slips the mirror back inside his shirt. He turns to his wife, bows once and proceeds on his journey off SL. *(Music)*

Wife

Totally amazed and still frightened, comes out from behind the tree to DSC, peering at the fleeing bandit. She turns to see her husband is fast leaving her behind, turns again to look at the bandit now offstage, almost leaps in fright at seeing him, and, arms extended, hurries off SL to catch up.

(Lights fade to blackout. Music swells for quick scene change. The tree and stump are simply exchanged.)

Scene 4:

(Suitable music could continue throughout scene.)

Boatman
Discovered on stage SL, unties an imaginary rope from around the tree and coils it as he gently pulls other end in. He throws the coil onto the bow of the boat.

He handles the gunwale until the boat is in position, and steps over and into the boat. The motion of a boat on water is indicated by the movement of his knees.

He bends and lifts his pole. He pushes off and poles his boat to SR using a heel-toe shuffle to move laterally. The young man and his wife enter SL.

Young Man
Hails the boatman with an uplifted arm.

Boatman
Responds by raising his arm and manoeuvring his boat back to SL.

Young Man
Bends and holds the gunwale to steady the boat for his wife to board.

Wife
Daintily steps over gunwale near the centre of the boat.

Young Man
Jumps into the boat; all three pick up the rocking movement of the boat he has just caused.

Boatman
Indicates with his cupped hand that payment is required.

Young Man
Automatically puts his hand into his empty pocket, and then looks dismayed, realizing he has forgotten to bring any coins. He looks to the boatman with a helpless gesture.

Boatman
Indicates he'd like to see what is wrapped up in the shirt.

Young Man
Takes out the mirror, bows three times, and passes it to his wife.

Wife
Quickly, but daintily, sticks out her tongue at the hated object and turns her head away as she passes it to the boatman.

Boatman
Looking dumbfounded at her reaction, accepts the mirror and slowly turns it to look into it. His blank expression gradually becomes a wide grin; a most comical-looking man grins back at him. The grin turns into a chuckle, and he points to it with one hand, by now splitting his sides with laughter. Eventually he passes the mirror back down the line and waves off any offer of payment.

He picks up his pole, and, in concert, the three cross the stage, moving with the movements of the boat. All the while, the boatman chuckles to himself.

Wife
Passing the mirror to her husband, haughtily combs her hair.

Young Man
Carefully positions the mirror inside his shirt under his arm. They arrive at SR and he jumps out and steadies the boat.

Wife
Daintily steps ashore. Husband and wife bow their thanks to the boatman and exit SR.

Boatman
Still chuckling, waves to them and poles back as

(Lights fade to black. Music swells to cover scene change.)

Scene 5:

(Lights up low key.)

Wise Elder
Discovered sitting in a lotus position US of a low urn-like devotional altar, head bowed, hands in a prayerful attitude. He raises his head, takes an imaginary taper from the urn, and lights the candles to the left and right of the urn.

(Lights dim up.)

Young Man
Arriving SR, US of the centre entrance, slips off his slippers, comes down stage and stands just to the right of the Elder.

Wife
Following, slips her slippers off and comes down just to the left of the Elder.

Elder
Looks up R, acknowledging the husband with slight nod. He turns and indicates "be seated" to the wife.

Young Man & Wife
Both bow deeply and sit in a similar lotus fashion.

Elder
Turns to the husband, dignified, expectant, inquisitive.

Young Man
Overcoming his feelings of awe, and with a slight start, remembers his mission. He withdraws the mirror, bows three quick, ritual bows and passes it to the Elder.

Elder
Accepts the mirror with a slight appraising smile, looks into it, and, holding it at a distance for better focus, succumbs to a moment of vanity, smoothing his hair. With a guilty start, he passes it back, nodding his approval.

Young Man
Accepts the mirror with both hands, bows and turns to look at the Elder.

Elder
Understanding, smiles faintly, nods a nod of comprehension, takes the husband's left hand and places it on the husband's own cheek.

Young Man
Looking at his reflection, ripples his fingers. Quickly he looks at his fingers, rippling them again. He places them on his cheek and looks in the mirror. He ripples them again, twice (interrupted only by a quick glance at his wife). A big smile of understanding comes over his face. He can hardly contain himself. Still

looking in the mirror and feeling very pleased, he crosses to his wife. Kneeling at her left, he begins to show her what the mirror does.

Wife
As her husband proffers the mirror, quickly and petulantly turns her head away.

Young Man
Holding mirror in his left hand, he gently but persistently places his right hand on her right cheek and draws her head around to look into the mirror.

Wife
Looks and, as her husband takes his right hand away, quickly takes his hand and places it back on her cheek, looking into the mirror, then at his hand, and back into the mirror. Confident now, she takes it, and, in wonder and pleasure, strokes her hair.

Young Man
Tweaks her nose.

Wife
Smiles back at her husband and tweaks her own nose.

Young Man
Beginning to get impatient, takes the mirror rather brusquely and stands up. He bows reverently to the Elder and backs off a step.

Wife
Realising the interview is over, stands, bows and also backs off.

Young Man
Bows again and goes to retrieve his slippers.

Wife
Emulates her husband, bowing again and following him out. *(Music)*

Young Man
Makes a final bow from the entrance and exits right.

Wife
A phrase behind, hastens to put on her slippers and follow.

Elder

With an almost impercetible shrug and a warm smile of understanding, adopts a more serious but peaceful expression and goes into meditation.

(Lights dim to black. Music swells for scene change.)

Scene 6:

(Lights up to reveal home scene. Low Key.)

Young Man

Arrives from SR, doffs his slippers, slides open the door, and comes through and down SR of C. He proceeds to admire himself in the mirror.

Wife

Following closely, slips off her slippers, steps through and closes the door. She goes to the lamp, pulls it down and turns the wick up. *(Lights dim up a little.)* She then goes to her husband's side and watches eagerly and with growing impatience.

Young Man

Holding the mirror in his left hand, explore his whole physiognomy, pinching his ear, lifting a tuft of hair, tweaking his nose, picking his teeth. Finally he gives the mirror to his wife.

Wife

Who has been in a high state of expectancy, literally snatches the mirror and turns away slightly, admiring herself, stroking her hair, shaping her eyebrows, flashing smiles.

Young Man

Impatiently grasps his wife's wrist with his left hand and, shaping the other side of the mirror with his right hand, indicates a pull, a resistance and a fumble. The mirror smashes to the floor at their feet. They stand, frozen, for an instant. He realizes that his toy is smashed and, irately, half turns his back to his wife to control his anger.

Wife

Believing herself responsible for the breaking of the mirror, wilts contritely and turns slightly away.

Young Man

Looks at the mirror on the floor, and then up at his wife. Realizing that she is blaming herself completely, he turns to face her and, with his downstage hand, gently strokes her face, lifts her head and draws her around to face him. *(Music)* With both hands, he outlines her face slowly, halo-like, starting with the top of her forehead and finishing at her chin.

Wife

Brings her hands up to take his as he finishes touching her face. They stand, motionless in tableau, smiling into each others eyes.

(Fade to blackout.)

Glossary

Accent: To accentuate or emphasize a rhythmic moment within the flow of an executed movement. In mime, the accent almost always occurs at the beginning and end of a movement. See also Clic, Toc and Dynamic.

Actor's Belief: A controlled state of mind in which the actor induces a belief within himself and, by projection, in the characters he and others portray. It draws on his real life experience and on his imagination. This belief includes belief in the environment that the stage purports to be; a belief in the declared passage of time; everything in the playwright's intention, as if it were all true. At the same time, the actor is very much aware that all is fiction.

Beat: A moment of time, long or short, within the rhythmic context of a situation.

Centre of Gravity: Nearly synonymous with centre of mass or centre of inertia; that point about which the body is in equilibrium in all positions. In order to maintain balance in a controlled movement, one must anticipate and compensate for a continual change in the centre of gravity.

Circumstances: A given set of conditions which influence the conduct of a character in attaining his objective in a given situation. See the teachings of Constantin Stanislavsky.

Clic: The accentuated muscular energy released at the beginning of and contained at the end of a physical phrase. See also Accent, Dynamic.

Commedia dell'Arte: A form of theatre, for the most part improvised, which flourished in Italy for three hundred years. Neglected since the Eighteenth Century, it is obscene, vulgar, mimetic, and acrobatic. Popular stock characters evolved over the years and influence playwrights to this day.

Delineation: To describe accurately an imaginary object by means of physical movements indicating its characteristics and use.

Double Take: See Take.

Double Shuffle: A heel-toe technique of moving the feet sideways to create the illusion that the spot upon which one is standing is moving.

Dynamic: Characterized by energy or effective action. Used here to describe all degrees of intensity, even stillness (static action). See also Accent and Clic.

Economy of Movement: One of the main principles of mime. Only those actions which advance the basic idea should be used. Too much embellishment spoils the effect.

Fixed Point: A technique in manipulation and movement where the body or a part of the body remains in a particular attitude fixed in space, or fixed in a spatial relationship to another real point or imaginary point, whether fixed or moving.

Focus (Actors):   The ability of the actor to focus his eyes on an imaginary object, whether near or far. It is strongly related to the actor's belief.

Generalize: Using a technique in a more rapid, less exacting detailed manner in order to suggest the passage of theatrical time or distance and to avoid tedium.

Grimace: The over-use of facial muscles in order to communicate the character's inner state; usually used to indicate a derogatory reaction.

Inner State: The thoughts, feelings and emotions evoked within the character by a particular set of circumstances.

Isolation: The ability to call on one muscle to perform a function in isolation from surrounding muscles and to separate one muscle or group of muscles from others. The separation of movement in one part moves the other parts minimally, if at all.

Leading Centre: That part of the body which leads or dominates the thrust of a movement.

Mobile Illusion: An illusory technique that involves lateral movement. (See Static Illusion.)

Muscle Contraction: The drawing of the muscles together in their length and breadth. It is always followed by a relaxation of the muscles.

Muscle Elongation: A state beyond relaxation where the muscles stretch and expand in length and breadth. Again, it is always followed by a relaxation of the muscles.

Muscle Memory: The learned muscle response to any repeated mental command to execute a movement. Association with repeated practice in the past allows the muscles to respond immediately, with minimal mental awareness.

Muscle Tone: The firm, sound, resilient condition of the muscle tissue in a vital body. "Tone" is also used here instead of the verb "tense," because of the psychological connotations of the latter term.

Neutral State: That physical and mental state of well-being and preparedness which enables one to be still in a meaningful way, or from which a meaningful action may emanate.

Objective: The fundamental purpose of the character within a unit of the play, characterized by action. The objective is technically defined by the words "I wish," followed by a verb of action. See, again, the teachings of Constantin Stanislavsky.

Outer State: The outer extension of the inner state. Our thoughts and feelings are transformed into an action which results from an initial set of circumstances.

Peripheral Vision: That extended area of sight to the far left and right, above and below the point at which we are consciously looking. It is the part of the total field of vision to which we normally give little attention. The awareness of it can be developed into an extremely useful tool for mime.

Physical Phrase: Verbal and written phrases require pauses and punctuation for clarity. In mime, too, we avoid slurring visual movements by means of pauses and accents, separating each phrase from every other.

Point of Levity: A surprisingly simple technique which helps one find a neutral basic position. An inner feeling of lightness escapes imaginatively through the collar bone area, drawing the mass of the body slightly upward into a relaxed, comfortable and vertical neutrality.

Purpose: See Objective.

Relate: A general term used to cover actions, reactions and interactions between characters, or between characters and objects in very subtle ways when more obvious specific actions are not required.

En Passant: Literally "in passing," the term corresponds in spoken theatre to the throw away line. It is usually an unconscious or possibly subconscious action made just before the actor is about to make a more obvious movement, but the result of such an action is generally major in effect.

Selectivity: See Economy of Movement.

Separation: See Isolation.

Shadow Movements: Accompany controlled conscious movement. Most everyone, without thought, develops certain personal mannerisms which may intrude on the meaningfulness of the major action. The mime must be aware of and eliminate these personal, superfluous shadow moves, in order that he may add those of the character.

Shaped Hand: The essence of an imaginary object is stated by the clarity of definition in the shaped hand. Before and after it defines the shape of the imaginary object, the hand must be as relaxed and unshaped as possible.

Shuffle Step: A locomotive heel-toe technique. One foot in moving to the side, is followed by a similar movement in the same direction by the other foot. See Double Shuffle.

Space Substance: To describe in a meaningful way the imaginary mass of an imaginary object.

Spatial Plane: The imaginary surface of flat objects. The surface can be vertical, as in the case of an imaginary wall, or horizontal, as in the case of a table top. The term may also refer to directional planes.

Specifics: Refers to the exact definition of an imaginary shape or the exact usage of an imaginary object, both in manipulation and illusion.

Stage Spike: A physical mark or spot, usually a small strip of tape, placed as a reference point on the stage. It is sometimes luminous if any part of the performance takes place in darkness.

Static Illusion: An illusion which does not move laterally, but is executed on the spot.

Take, Double Take: A casual, non-comprehending look (or two) towards a focal point and away, followed by comprehension and a rapid look of astonishment or disbelief back at the focal point. The head movement is most important in making a take or double take effective.

Toc: See Accent, Clic, and Dynamic.

Topography: The random markings on a stage such as cracks, joins, paint spots, etc. which can serve as reference points when the actor is furnishing the area with imaginary set pieces.

Bibliography

BARLANGHY, Istvan. *Mime: Training and Exercises.* London: The Imperial Society of Teachers of Dancing, 1967.

BLUNT, Jerry. *The Composite Art of Acting.* New York: The Macmillan Company, 1966.

DECROUX, Etienne. *Paroles sur le Mime.* Paris: Gallimard, 1963.

DORCY, Jean. *J'aime le Mime.* Paris: Deno el, (No date).
The Mime. New York: Robert Speller & Sons, 1961.

KIPNIS, Claude. *The Mime Book.* New York: Harper and Row, 1974.

KLINE, Peter, and MEADORSS, Nancy. *Physical Movement for the Theatre.* New York: Richards and Rosen Press, 1971.

LABAN, Rudolf. *The Mastery of Movement.* London: Macdonald and Evans Ltd., 1961.

LAWSON, Joan. *Mime.* London: Pitman & Sons Ltd., 1957.

NICOLL, Allardyce. *Masks, Mimes and Miracles.* New York: Cooper Square Publishers Inc., 1963.

PENROD, James. *Movement for the Performing Artists.* Palo Alto, California: Mayfield Publishing Co., 1974.

ROLFE, Bari. *Commedia dell'Arte: A Scene Study Book.* San Francisco: Persona Products, 1977.
Behind the Mask. San Francisco: Persona Products, 1977.

SAYRE, Gwendo. *Creative Miming.* London: Herbert Jenkins, 1959.

SHEPARD, Richmond. *Mime, The Technique of Silence.* New York: Drama Book Specialists, 1971.

SPOLIN, Viola. *Improvisation for the Theatre.* Evanston, Illinois: Northwestern University Press, 1970 (c 1963).

STANISLAVSKY, Constantin. *An Actor Prepares.* New York: Theatre Art Books, 1966. (21st printing).